THEOLOGY
and
CONTEMPORARY
ART FORMS

JOHN P. NEWPORT

WORD BOOKS, PUBLISHER
Waco, Texas—London, England

Printed in the United States of America.
Library of Congress Catalog Card Number: 75-134940

TO
EDDIE BELLE

Preface

When a member of the theological community seeks to discuss the contemporary arts, he often finds himself in a defensive position in relation to his colleagues and constituency and to any artists who might be interested. As is pointed out in chapter I, in the Christian tradition there has long been a suspicion of the artist and his work. This is especially true in recent years since the majority of the artists are no longer serving the established interests of the churches. In fact, the arts have sought and largely gained autonomy. The artists, in turn, are now suspicious of any attempt by theology to question their autonomy or seek to give what is called "outside" interpretation.

Despite the problems involved, it is still seen by this writer as important for theologians of differing theological backgrounds to become involved in evaluation in the area of the arts. It is hoped that the result is not just an uninformed theological prejudgment. Obviously the viewpoint of a theologian will be colored by his background and faith commitment. In this study, however, there has been an attempt at a sensitive probing and listening to what the artists have to say.

Since presuppositions are profoundly influenced by background and training, it is important and should be helpful to the reader to relate in some detail relevant background data. The writer's interest in formal study in theology and the contemporary arts arose in periods of graduate study at the University of Edinburgh in Scotland and at the University of Basel in Switzerland. A sabbatical year at Harvard University provided an opportunity for crystallization of this interest. Especially helpful during this period were Samuel Miller, Paul Tillich, George Buttrick, John Wild, and Joseph Fletcher. A second sabbatical in New York City at Union Theological Seminary furnished a further opportunity to continue formal study in the area of the arts. Helpful during this sabbatical period were Tom Driver and John Macquarrie, as well as the personnel at the New York museums. Additional periods of study in New York were stimulating in terms of study programs under the leadership of Al Carmines and Harvey Cox. Roger Ortmayer, formerly of Perkins School of Theology, Southern Methodist University, and now secretary of the Department of Church and Culture of the National Council of the Churches of Christ, furnished valuable assistance in the inauguration of courses in "Theology and the Arts" at the seminary level.

Material found in these chapters has been developed in the course of lectures and addresses at numerous colleges and universities. Especially meaningful has been the interest in "Theology and the Contemporary Arts" among lay people in various national laymen's meetings and local churches.

The immediate occasion of the more precise formulation of these materials was the invitation to deliver the Norton Lectures at the Southern Baptist Theological Seminary, Louisville, Kentucky in November, 1969. Appreciation is expressed to President Duke McCall and the faculty for the invitation and to the faculty and students of the seminary for their attendance and interest in the lectures. Further stimulus for publishing and enlarging the lectures was provided by the invitation of Rice University, Houston, Texas to be a Visiting Professor in "Religion in the Arts" in 1971.

I am particularly grateful for the students, administration, and faculty of Southwestern Baptist Seminary, Fort Worth, Texas, who have provided a delightful context for study and research in this area. Appreciation is in order to Ann Roper, my secretary, who was always "ahead" of me in efficient manuscript typing and indexing. I also would like to thank Floyd Thatcher, Vice President and Executive Editor of Word Books, Inc., who extended the invitation to prepare the manuscript for publication. His perceptive and critical reading of the manuscript provided the basis for revision. Above all, I am grateful to my wife, Eddie Belle, who not only read and gave advice on the manuscript, but also encouraged me to stay with it when my "practical temperament" would beckon toward something less rigorous.

Contents

I

THEOLOGY AND CONTEMPORARY
ART FORMS

Introduction

WE ARE IN THE MIDST of an "art explosion."[1] It is now recognized that societies live by their symbols or myths, in the sense of compelling world-pictures and their assumptions. They order their institutions and unwritten laws by these symbols.

The controversial critic, Susan Sontag, claims that contemporary art forms are unifying our culture and modifying our sensibility or consciousness. She maintains that the new cinema, painting, music, and literature are so powerful that they give rise to something like an exultation, commitment, and captivation.[2] Thus the artist and the image-maker play a decisive role—for good or evil.

Why would a professional or lay theologian investigate art forms? Isn't theology restricted to its own revealed materials? In seeking to answer these questions, it should be remembered

---

[1]John P. Newport, "God, Man and Redemption in Modern Art," *Review and Expositor,* LXI (Summer, 1964), p. 143.
[2]Susan Sontag, *Against Interpretation* (New York: Dell Publishing Co., Inc., 1961), pp. 293-304.

that theology is a labor of the human mind in which an attempt is made to understand the relations between God and the world. The fact that the focal point is the final revelation in Jesus Christ does not lessen the need to understand God's relation to the world.

There are three major sources of understanding for a contemporary theologian, professional or lay. One source is the Bible, which is regulative. The second is doctrinal teaching in previous Christian history. The third source is reason. And reason must have context and relatedness. This context comes from experience. For the theologian there are three types of experience. First, there is personal experience, including his own history. Second, there is the historical experience of the communities to which he belongs, including his church, nation, and other social groups. The third is cultural experience.[3]

Cultural experience is so vast and general that it must be made specific in order for it to have meaning. The artists are those who have gifts, skills, intuitions, and depth of understanding related to the human scene. An artist is a communicator who captures a small part of human experience in an attempt to express the greater part.

There are many "taste-makers," including critics, essayists, and philosophers, but in the contemporary age, the artist shapes and focuses shared human life in the most available and powerful way. In fact, some of the metaphors and allegories of the artists are so intense and urgent that they literally overwhelm society.[4] If the theologian remains aloof from the work of the artists, he is ignoring the world which theology attempts to understand in relation to God.

[3]Indebtedness to lectures and discussion in classes in "Doctrines of Man in Modern Drama," Professor Tom Driver, Union Theological Seminary, New York City, 1965, is acknowledged.

[4]John P. Newport, "Questions Ministers Ask About Contemporary Literature and Drama," *Southwestern Journal of Theology*, Vol. 10 (Spring, 1968), pp. 31f.

Cf. also Nathan Scott, Jr., *Craters of the Spirit* (Washington: Corpus Books, 1968), p. 19. Indebtedness to lectures and discussion in classes in "Religion and Literature," Professor Samuel Miller, Harvard University, 1958-59, is acknowledged.

Reasons for the Divorce Between Theology and the Arts

Unfortunately, for many reasons, there has been a frightful divorce between theology and the arts. And where there has been a relationship, the aesthetic standards of most theologians have been low. Many of the pictures on the walls, the books on the shelves, and the records played are products of a sentimental, pietistic dilution of aesthetic integrity. A survey of religious poetry and hymnody revealed trite theological truth expressed in rhyme with a tendency to use nineteenth-century idioms. Religious novels studied showed superficial and unreal characters engaged in stock situations. Evidently, some theologians think that imagination is intrinsically evil and so revert to cliché and custom.[5]

At a recent Arts Festival, young theologians reveled in controversial paintings, experimental music, aesthetic dances, and avant-garde movies. Some older theologians did not look at the striking colors, grotesque shapes, and dissonant sounds with uncritical appreciation. At first I harbored resentment toward these critical friends. Then I began to think seriously about *why* our Protestant forefathers viewed the arts with deep suspicion. The great frontier evangelist, Charles Finney, first president of Oberlin College, referred to all dramatists and actors as "a host of triflers and blasphemers of God." In the more recent past, prominent theologians have treated theater-going as a mere extension of the biblical view of "chambering and wantonness."[6] I remember the negative statements about art forms given during youth forums.

As will be noted, much of the hostility of eighteenth and nineteenth-century churches toward aesthetic experience reflected an other-worldliness and anti-life theology which is largely anti-biblical. On the other hand, there is a sense in which the artistic enterprises participate in and focalize the human rebellion against God. There is a long tradition in the arts which assigns them ultimate autonomy and makes creativ-

---

[5]Frank E. Gaebelein, "Toward a Biblical View of Aesthetics," *Christianity Today*, (August 30. 1968), p. 1122.

[6]E. William Muehl, "The Aesthetic Heresy," *Reflection* (November, 1968), p. 1.

ity its own law. Like every other manifestation of human activity, artistic impulses can become the media of self-destruction and the corruption of other people. In fact, artistic genius may have even greater possibilities for demonic influence than the less gifted person.

Literary and dramatic artists, for example, have complete control over both the internal development of their characters and the context of that development. In the writing of history, objective data keeps statements under some kind of control. It can be shown that Louis XVI was not a genius at statecraft and Marilyn Monroe was not a withered hag. But in art, the artist is a god. He is master of both character and continuity. He can make villains exciting and good men dull. Look what he has done to ministers! He can show rakes full of compassion and make faithful husbands objects of ridicule. The artist can mix the component elements of life in unrealistic and even irresponsible ways. Oftentimes, however, a person is called an "antiquarian" if he even suggests that the world of creative imagination is also deeply involved in the general corruption of man.[7]

Great artists do have originality and express their personal visions, but they also keep some rapport with common humanity and reality. The most dangerous atheism is the claim that reality is wholly defined by my vision and subject to my manipulation. Because an artist has peculiar abilities, he also has the special danger of repeating the sin of the Garden of Eden. Only God can say, "I am that I am."[8]

Most people will concede that art has done its part in creating the divorce between theology and the arts. We have pointed out that theologians should be wary. On the other hand, theologians should accept their share (which is large) of the blame for the divorce. Theologians have exhibited narrowness, rigidity, and low aesthetic standards, and there has been theological imperialism rather than sensitive probing and listening to what the artist has to say. During the last hundred years, many of the significant movements in the arts

---

[7]Ibid, pp. 1,2.
[8]Ibid., p. 4.

have been rejected by the churches. But now I believe that theologians should take the initiative in seeking a reunion. It is their business to forgive.

Fortunately, there are examples of artistic creativity and achievements and appreciation in Christian history. The biblical writers were in many cases flexible and appreciative of contemporary cultural developments. They oftentimes adapted and utilized these cultural forms. The early Fathers, Scholastics, and the Reformers were in many cases bold, strong, and creative.

Reasons for the Contemporary Theological Interest in the Arts

One of the significant recent innovations in the teaching of theology on the American scene is the inclusion of studies in the arts in the context of the theological curriculum itself.[9] I had the privilege of participating in the first national meeting of "The Fellowship of Christians in the Arts, Media and Entertainment" at Palm Springs, California. Journals and books are readily available in this area. Social scientists, such as Donald Meyer, have noted the extent to which the arts are arousing the attention of American Protestantism.[10] The American Academy of Religion has a section in each annual meeting which is concerned with "Art, Literature, and Religion."

This theological emphasis has not been developed just to stimulate interest in theological studies, as some have implied.[11] In addition to those already mentioned, there are several significant reasons why theology should give serious concern to the arts.

The *first* reason is related to the biblical teaching that God reveals and carries on his redemptive purpose in the concrete actualities of time and history.[12]

In the Old Testament, God called for his people to live in

---

[9]Nathan A. Scott, Jr., *Negative Capability* (New Haven: Yale University Press, 1968), p. 45.
[10]Cf. Donald B. Meyer, *The Protestant Search for Political Realism: 1919-1941* (Berkeley: University of California Press, 1960).
[11]Scott, *Negative Capability,* p. 146.
[12]Ibid., p. 149.

and work out his purpose in history. In the New Testament, this emphasis is continued. In other words, the world is the concrete historical context where that which is transcendental and ultimate can be experienced. The Christian community, therefore, cannot cut itself off from the characteristic artistic vitalities of history—past and present. The interest in the arts by the theologian is not an unprincipled whoring after what is momentarily prestigious in the cultural establishment. This interest springs, rather, from a meaningful recovery of a basic biblical emphasis. The Bible demands that the theologian move out into a lover's quarrel with the world. Theology must engage in a dialogue with the arts. It must define itself and understand itself in relation to the arts as well as psychology, science, sociology, and other humanistic disciplines.[13]

The Old Testament records how the covenant community defined and understood itself in relation to the literature of Babylon and Canaan and the wisdom tradition of Egypt and Edom. The pagan literature and vitalities of Hellenism were transubstantiated by the early church. In John, Hebrews, and Ephesians, Christianity absorbed and surmounted the pagan literature of meaninglessness. The mood and kerygmatic witness of the early church was of a pitch and level to encounter, master, and transmute to its own purposes the dynamic conceptions of pagan antiquity. The early Christians lived by a creative power and ideology that outrivaled the seven wonders of the world.[14]

It was in the conflict of world-views that Israel and then Christianity drew resources of language to define and communicate themselves. Today the realities of contemporary art forms provide challenge, provocation, and nourishment to the theological enterprise. Even as the Apostle Paul said that God's work among the Gentiles would provoke the Jews, so today many see God using artists to provoke and needle the Christian movement.[15]

---

[13]Ibid., p. 160. Cf. also Dietrich Bonhoeffer, *Letters and Papers from Prison,* trans. by Reginald H. Fuller and ed. by Eberhard Bethage (London: SCM Press Ltd., 1953).

[14]Amos N. Wilder, "Art and Theological Meaning," *Union Seminary Theological Review* (November, 1962), p. 40.

[15]Ibid., p. 40.

Before further discussion, it should be noted that there are real dangers for the theologian in this new interest in the arts. Some young theologians (and some not so young) have gone into an uncritical "eros" or passion and have made a fetish of creative spontaneity without biblical norms. They are much like the Jewish youths of the Seleucid period in interbiblical times. I and II Maccabees record that the young Jews were completely captivated by things which were Greek. They wore Greek clothes, went to the circus and theater, and were ashamed of their circumcision. They had been inhibited by the rigidities of the period of the Second Temple. In contrast, the Greek humanism seemed exciting. And so today! We react to the rigidities of our middle-class Protestant background and are attracted by the vitality and exuberance of the arts.[16]

Some young theologians turn from Pietism to Romanticism. They are fascinated by the religious dance, mystical poetry, and sentimental painting[17] and are attracted to painters Paul Klee and Salvador Dali, who have turned to Christian symbols to portray their recent pantheistic mysticism. They are drawn to the later Heidegger, who finds the poetry of Rilke and Hölderlin a mouthpiece of the impersonal "what is" (being).

Other theologians come from a dogmatic tradition involving a built-in asceticism or emotional barrenness. The temptation here is to turn to some kind of Christian antinomianism or neglect of norms. Or there may be an interest in a sophisticated high-church symbolic traditionalism. The antinomian reaction sometimes takes people out of organized church life as in the case of André Gide or Robert Graves.[18]

However, we are more concerned here with the benefits of a wise confrontation with the arts than with the misunderstandings and possible harmful reactions.

A *second* reason for the theologian to be concerned with the arts is related to the fact that the arts give a peculiarly

---

[16]Ibid., p. 40f. Cf. also Amos N. Wilder, *The New Voice* (New York: Herder and Herder, 1969), pp. 235-263.
[17]Ibid., p. 41.
[18]Ibid.

direct access to the distinctive tone, concerns, and feelings of a given culture.[19]

The artists not only mirror their age in its subtlest nuances, but they generally do it a generation ahead of more abstract and theoretical thinkers. Thus, art has an unusual capacity to document the time-spirit. It gives the theologian an indispensable kind of index to the actual world to be addressed. Cézanne, at the beginning of the twentieth century, saw and painted space in a new way—as a spontaneous totality. He painted the *being* of space rather than its *measurements* and encompassed far and near in one totality. He told us that the *old* world of mechanics was gone and we must *now* live in the *new* world of spaces. This new world transcends cause and effect.[20]

How is this time-documentation useful for theology? The whole discussion of a doctrine such as death, for example, must be correlated with the form in which death presents itself to the contemporary mind. Subtle changes have profoundly altered man's outlook and sensibility in regard to death. These changes affect even those who cherish traditional religious images. The older view which could be used by Tennyson, Browning, Emerson, Francis Thompson, and Vachel Lindsay is now almost obsolete and hardly authentic for our time.[21]

In thinking of death, contemporary people are no longer just concerned with a transition from one level of existence to another. A more radical concern is before us now. It is not just a passage from something to something else. The more basic question is being raised—is there any meaning at all— now or ever? Contemporary art forms point out that our confrontation with nothingness no longer waits upon the moment of death. Meaninglessness, vacancy, and non-being have to be dealt with here and now. The bomb, war, geno-

[19]Scott, *Negative Capability,* p. 163.
[20]Rollo May, *Love and Will* (New York: W. W. Norton and Co., Inc., 1969), pp. 322f.
[21]Amos Wilder, "Mortality and Contemporary Literature," *The Modern Vision of Death,* ed. Nathan Scott (Richmond, Va.: John Knox Press, 1967), p. 22. Cf. also Wilder, *The New Voice,* pp. 216f.

cide, and the survival of the race reverberate in our innermost beings.

Rainer Maria Rilke was one of the first, in his poetry, who wrote of the idea of life as interpenetrated with death. Ernest Hemingway and William Faulkner force us to see death in a similar way, as does William Butler Yeats. Eugene O'Neill sees death as having priority over life. Dylan Thomas in his poem, *Twenty-four Years,* speaks of our being "dressed to die" already at our birth. The early Heidegger reflects this view in philosophy. Samuel Beckett and Eugene Ionesco contend that life itself is absurd and meaningless.[22]

Before any discussion of life beyond death becomes meaningful today, the prior problem of despair, absurdity, chaos, and meaninglessness must be understood and addressed. To such a need, the early New Testament church spoke. The heart of its affirmation revolved around the resurrection of Christ and the inauguration of a new quality of life. Christ brings a meaning here and now—a meaning which will continue and be enlarged and fulfilled beyond death.

A *third* reason for theology to be concerned with the arts is because the arts focalize (in a remarkably vivid and startling way) on the vital issues and themes which are the central concern of theology.[23]

Artists are probing anew in spirited and original ways the issues of ultimate concern with which theology has perennially dealt. Denis de Rougement points out that an authentic work of art is an "oriented or calculated trap for meditation." It magnetizes the sensibility. It fascinates to meditation.[24] An art form focuses the attention upon an issue or theme which transcends the art form itself. Authentic art demands that we pause, however briefly, for the purpose of disclosure or disturbance. Pablo Picasso defines art as "a lie that makes us

---

[22]Ibid., p. 19.
[23]Scott, *Negative Capability*, p. 161.
[24]Denis de Rougemont, "Religion and the Mission of the Artist," in *Spiritual Problems in Contemporary Literature*, ed. Stanley R. Hopper, (New York: Harper and Brothers, 1952), p. 176.

realize the truth." Artists work to devise symbolic break-throughs by which neglected or forgotten themes and realities become important again.[25]

To put it another way, art forms raise not only questions, but Christian *themes*. Arthur Miller's *All My Sons* deals with guilt. The theme of the relation of sin and death is found in *All the King's Men* by Robert Penn Warren. Has anyone dealt with original sin or the pervasiveness of evil in a more power-ful way than has William Golding in the *Lord of the Flies?*

In our desacralized world, what was once the religious di-mension is opened up for many by artistic experience alone. And it is done at the deep level of feeling and passion.

In the *fourth* place, the arts help to spell out in a dramatic fashion the implications of various world-views. They help to prepare the way for a clearer representation of life options. By way of contrast and dialogue, they help theology to de-velop its own self-knowledge and inner clarity.[26]

When a work of art, a literary work, for example, is seen as a totality, it spells out a fundamental attitude or orientation toward the world. It has a "blik."[27] The author projects a model of life by which experience may be ordered and inter-preted. This projection or development is not done in an ab-stract or rational way. Rather, a given perspective is "fleshed out" and dramatized through a vibrant pattern of living im-ages. It catches fish that the more rational nets do not get.[28]

Northrop Frye suggests that literature bears something of the same relationship to theology that mathematics bears to the physical sciences. The pure mathematician proceeds by making postulates and assumptions and seeing what comes out of them. The poet, the novelist, and the dramatist vitalize

---

[25]Roger Hazelton, *A Theological Approach to Art* (New York: Abing-don Press, 1967), p. 21.

[26]Nathan A. Scott, Jr., "Introduction: Theology and the Literary Imagina-tion," in *Adversity and Grace*, ed. Nathan A. Scott, Jr. (Chicago: The University of Chicago Press, 1968), pp. 20f.

[27]"Blik" is a neologism invented by the English philosopher, R. M. Hare, for the sake of specifying what theological discourse is "about." It seeks to give a perspective on life.

[28]Scott, "Introduction: Theology and the Literary Imagination," p. 23.

meditation on matters of ultimate concern by making concrete the real meaning of a given life-orientation. They "dance out" the real implications of various perspectives. They do experimental theology. The artist shows how a particular faith or life-orientation really *looks* under the full stress of experience. Faulkner's strange style is appropriate to the ruined world that his novels portray. The bare simplicity of Hemingway's style reveals the basic stoicism of his moral vision. The experimental work of the artist thus helps to prevent theology from becoming merely formal, superficial, and irrelevant.[29]

Francis A. Schaeffer, the conservative apologist, points out the importance of the arts in spelling out the implications of various world-views or sets of presuppositions. The following examples are used by Schaeffer to illustrate his thesis. Sartre's novels and dramas end in the conclusion that we live in an absurd universe. Nevertheless, we try to authenticate ourselves by an act of the will. It does not really matter in which direction we act as long as we act. Paul Gauguin tried to find a humanistic universal. He went to Tahiti and there championed the idea of the noble savage, the return to the primitive, as the source of the universal. But in his comments on his last great painting, *What? Whence? Whither?*, he showed his despair. In *The Silence* Ingmar Bergman, the Swedish movie director, according to Schaeffer, spells out the meaning of utter nihilism. Man does not even have the hope of authenticating himself by an act of the will. The movie is a series of snapshots—unrelated—click, click, click—with no meaning or moral. John Cage proposes and composes music born of chance and indeterminancy. He uses mechanical conductors. He gets a clue from the Chinese system of tossing coins or yarrow sticks. His music dramatically outlines what it means to believe in an impersonal universe which speaks through blind chance.[30]

For Schaeffer, this "spelling out" of the implications of alternative world-views prepares the way for an understanding

---

[29]Scott, *Negative Capability,* p. 166.
[30]Francis A. Schaeffer, *The God Who Is There* (Chicago: Inter-Varsity Press, 1968), pp. 30-43.

of the uniqueness of the Christian view. The "spelling out" also helps men to see the real meaning and the weaknesses and strengths of alternative world-views. After such a "spelling out" of the options, the door is often open for a new appreciation and acceptance of the biblical option.[31]

A *fifth* statement should be made about the relation of theology and the arts. Both the professional and lay theologian must evaluate and interpret the arts in terms of biblical criteria.

Much appreciation has been expressed for the arts in these comments. But the very power of the arts and the imagination calls for a rigorous Christian discrimination. Art often takes the form of idols. There are false imaginations. As has been noted, great societies and civilizations live by their myths, their compelling world-pictures. The most powerful influences in creating and popularizing these myths are the artists, the image-makers. But the theologian must finally take a stand. He must finally push beyond sensitive listening and looking.[32]

There are some artists and art critics who tend to cut art forms off from the broader world beyond their own style and syntax boundaries. The view of this group of theorists is called "The New Criticism." For this group the artist's vision is not fully formed until it is objectified in a medium. The guiding principle of the creative process is derived from the medium to which the artist's metaphysic or perspective is submitted and by which it is controlled. The original idea is radically transformed by the medium. The artist trusts his medium, and it will bring meaning to birth. The artist is thus a certain kind of technician. His work of art does not lead us beyond himself into some external realm of meaning.[33] The work of art is wholly self-contained, pointing neither outward to the general world or meaning nor inward to the artist's inner subjectiv-

---

[31]Ibid., pp. 126-130.
[32]Wilder, "Art and Theological Meaning," pp. 46f. Cf. also Richard E. Sherrell, *The Human Image: Avant-Garde and Christian* (Richmond, Va.: John Knox Press, 1969), p. 132.
[33]Nathan A. Scott, Jr, "The Collaboration of Vision in the Poetic Act: Its Establishment of the Religious Dimension," *The Christian Scholar*, XL (Dec., 1957), pp. 282f., 279.

ity.[34] Susan Sontag suggests that contemporary art is more interested in form than in content. It likes a literature, for example, which avoids interpretation. Such theorists have great anxiety about the purity of art forms, believing they are not to be contaminated by ideas.[35]

It is the contention of Nathan Scott, Richard Sherrell, and other theological critics, however, that poets, novelists, and playwrights do have ideas. By this the theological critics do not mean that the work of art is *merely* an expression of the artist's subjectivity or emotion. The emotionalist view would convert aesthetics into a branch of psychology.[36] These theological critics, following Erich Auerbach, are attentive to grammatical and syntactical structures and to diction. Upon the basis of this approach to a text, the vision of the artist is found as *inherent* in the artistic structure. The theological evaluation of a work of art must *begin* with a formal analysis.[37] Before evaluating ideas in the work of art, concern should be given to the density of experience and the nuances of feeling that the artist is able to actualize through these ideas. The integrity of the artistic text must be respected. Marxist critics are examples of such failure.[38]

However, granted the importance of formal artistic analysis, most theological critics contend that artists have a poetic vision which contains either a crypto-religious or philosophical dimension. This dimension operates in the creative act and inheres in the literary work, thus making theological evaluation a possibility as well as a necessity.[39]

Artists such as Blake, Goethe, Melville, Dostoevsky, and Ibsen did "think." The content of their thought deeply penetrates their distinctively poetic creations. Words have a refer-

---

[34]Scott, *Negative Capability,* p. 120.
[35]Sontag, *Against Interpretation,* p. 14.
[36]Nathan A. Scott, Jr., *The Broken Center:* Studies in the Theological Horizon of Modern Literature (New Haven: Yale University Press, 1966), p. 201.
[37]Scott, "Collaboration of Vision," p. 281.
[38]Nathan A. Scott, Jr., "The Relation of Theology to Literary Criticism," *The Journal of Religion,* XXXIII (October, 1953), p. 266f.
[39]Ibid., p. 269. Cf. also Northrup Frye, *Anatomy of Criticism: Four Essays* (Princeton: Princeton University Press, 1957), p. 7.

ential thrust beyond themselves to a world-view.[40] According
to Jacques Maritain, artistic statements are signs or expres-
sions of how the artist in his own "interiority" and vision
grasps the world and gives it order and meaning. At the root
of the creative process there is a profound act of creative intuition.[41]

Without minimizing the importance of the form of the literary work itself, it must be said that the work of art bears
testimony both to the artist's vision and to the surrounding
world of which it is a part. Despite the difference between the
"non-discursive" modalities of art and the "discursive" modalities of systematic thought, art and metaphysics do meet
and coalesce. Most great writers such as Dostoevsky, Lawrence, Kafka, Eliot, Camus, Beckett, Faulkner, and Bellow
are drenched in the stuff of ideas and world-views. Artists,
like philosophers and theologians, draw out the implications
of an experienced fragment of life.[42]

A Christian theologian, therefore, is always involved in a
war of myths or world-views for men's souls. It is important
that the theologian in any epoch should have ability and dynamic in the area of theological art criticism. Without violating the integrity of literary texts, he should be able to grasp
clearly the presuppositions of the various world-views presented by artists. He should be able to analyze these world-
views and note their implications.[43] He should then have the
capacity to evaluate these world-views in light of biblical
standards. In a more positive way, the theologian should be a
part of a Christian vanguard which would provide compelling

---

[40]Scott, *Craters of the Spirit*, p. 17. Cf. also Sherrell, *The Human Image*,
pp. 24-26.

[41]Sherrell, *The Human Image*, p. 26. Cf. Jacques Maritain, *Creative Intuition in Art and Poetry* (New York: Pantheon Books, 1953).

[42]Martin Turnell, *Modern Literature and Christian Faith* (Westminster,
Maryland: The Newman Press, 1961), p. 28; Philip Wheelright, *Metaphor
and Reality* (Bloomington: Indiana University Press, 1962), p. 167.

[43]The chief strategy which has unified serious literary criticism by Christian writers has involved the exploration and evaluation of the *world-views*
implicit in the significant literature of our period. Cf. Amos Wilder, *Modern
Poetry* (New York: Harper, 1940); Stanley Romaine Hopper, *The Crisis
of Faith* (New York: Abingdon, 1944) and *Spiritual Problems in Contemporary Literature,* ed. Stanley Romaine Hopper (New York: Harper,

images and potent art forms rooted in a biblical perspective.[44]

There are biblical precedents for these activities. In one sense, the biblical faith was a continual war against pagan myths and world-views. With the emergence of the gospel came a renewal of mythical and symbolic apprehension and communication. The new imagery, however, arose out of the drama of the Cross and Resurrection. The biblical faith was a world-view or world-portrayal that inevitably contradicted the imaginations of Greece and Rome, even as it borrowed from them and transfigured them.[45]

Thus, the first believers can give us guidelines as we enter our war of myths and seek to overthrow the false icons of our Romes and Corinths. The Christian artist and theologian learn that the power of conception is rooted in the first century Christian vision which includes the Cross and the Resurrection.[46] From these first believers, we learn that the Christian must speak to every man and age in his current idiom. There

---

1952); Brother George Every, *Christian Discrimination* (London: The Sheldon Press, 1940) and *Poetry and Personal Responsibility* (London: SCM Press, 1949); William Tiverton (Martin Jarrett-Kerr), *D. H. Lawrence and Human Existence* (London: Rockliff, 1951), *F. Mauriac* (Cambridge: Yale University Press, 1954) and Wladimir Weidle, *The Dilemma of the Arts* (London: SCM Press, 1948) trans. by Martin Jarrett-Kerr; S. L. Bethell, *The Literary Outlook and Essays on Literary Criticism* (London: Dennis Dobson Ltd., 1948); Jacques Maritain, *Art and Scholasticism* and *Creative Intuition in Art and Poetry;* Allen Tate, *The Forlorn Demon* (Chicago: Regnery, 1953) and W. K. Wimsatt, *The Verbal Icon* (Lexington: University of Kentucky Press, 1954).

[44]Wilder, "Art and Theological Meaning," p. 47.

[45]Ibid., p. 47.

[46]It is important that the contemporary theological interpreter utilize the total Christian vision, including creation, incarnation, history, cross, resurrection and eschatology. Some would see in Nathan Scott's strong emphasis on the Incarnation a relative neglect of the Atonement. However, Scott himself cautions the theological critic against making any Christian doctrine the single criterion of the Christian vision. Randall Stewart's use of the doctrine of Original Sin illustrates for Scott the inadequacy of such an approach. The manner in which Stewart (Cf. *American Literature and Christian Doctrine*, Baton Rouge: L.S.U. Press., 1958) employs this one doctrine suggests erroneously that "it furnishes a sufficient summation of the full Christian wisdom about human existence." Stewart also tends drastically to oversimplify "the actual complexity of the relation of Christianity to modern culture" (Nathan A. Scott, Jr., "Judgment Marked by a Cellar: The American Negro Writer and the Dialectic of Despair" in *The Shapeless God: Essays on Modern Fiction*, ed. by Harry J. Mooney, Jr. and Thomas F. Staley, n.p.: University of Pittsburgh Press, 1968, p. 142).

is the further lesson of the importance of "bodying forth" rather than emphasizing abstract instruction and argument.[47]

Representative Theological Approaches to the Arts

How do representative theologians and Christian artists approach this evaluative task? Some utilize what has been called the "religious amiability" approach. The arts of today primarily reflect alienation, and this alienation can be seen as a preparation for the gospel. Works of art also utilize non-religious symbols to point to the infinite source of the finite. Paul Tillich, Nathan Scott, and Amos Wilder utilize this approach according to Sallie TeSelle.[48]

Another approach by theologians or religiously oriented critics is known as "Christian discrimination."[49] It is critical and judgmental toward any culture or artistic manifestation that is not either specifically or latently Christian. This approach concentrates on the degree to which the beliefs and morals projected in a work of art are aligned with Christian standards. The principal theoreticians of this criterion include such well-known critics as T. E. Hulme, T. S. Eliot, Cleanth Brooks, and Randall Stewart.[50] Other men who utilize a similar approach are R. W. B. Lewis, F. W. Dillistone, John Killinger, and Francois Mauriac.[51]

---

[47]Wilder, "Art and Theological Meaning," p. 47.

[48]Sallie McFague TeSelle, *Literature and the Christian Life* (New Haven: Yale University Press, 1966), pp. 8-15.

[49]Ibid., pp. 16-19.

[50]Cf. T. E. Hulme, ed. by Herbert Read, *Speculations: Essays on Humanism and the Philosophy of Art* (New York: Harcourt, Brace and Company, 1924); T. S. Eliot, *After Strange Gods: A Primer of Modern Heresy* (London: Faber and Faber, Ltd., 1934); Cleanth Brooks, *The Hidden God: Studies in Hemingway, Faulkner, Yeats, Eliot and Warren* (New Haven: Yale University Press, 1963); and Randall Stewart, *American Literature and Christian Doctrine* (Baton Rouge: Louisiana State University Press, 1958).

[51]Cf. R.W.B. Lewis, *The Picaresque Saint: Representative Figures in Contemporary Fiction* (London: Victor Gollancz, Ltd., 1956); F. W. Dillistone, *The Novelist and the Passion Story* (New York: Sheed and Ward, 1960); John Killinger, *The Failure of Theology in Modern Literature* (New York: Abingdon Press, 1963); and Francois Mauriac, *God and Mammon* (London: Sheed and Ward, 1936).

Those theologians who attempt to construct Christian presuppositions are designated as utilizing an approach called "Christian aesthetics." William F. Lynch represents this stance.[52]

Critics such as Roland M. Frye, Erich Heller, and Erich Auerbach are difficult to classify. They are sometimes called the "old critics."[53]

It would be helpful to give in somewhat more detail the approach of selected theologians. John Maguire describes his approach as "coping with chaos." He would discount the life-style of the "aesthete" who attempts to cope with life by transcending it through fancy and fantasy. The way of the "victim" is inadequate because it attempts to cope with life by absorbing the world or yielding oneself to the world. The way of the "aggressor" attempts to assault life into submission. For Maguire, the way of "revelation" takes artistic styles and transfigures them by elevating their strengths and muting their weaknesses under biblical guidance and power. Here are helpful hints for the theologian-critic.[54]

For Chad Walsh, a theologian must acquire a pair of Christian metaphorical eyes through which he can gain perspective.[55] Edmund Fuller's approach to the problem of contemporary art forms is in terms of the question, "What is the artist's view of man? How does it compare with the normative Judaeo-Christian view?"[56]

Nathan Scott calls for a vigorous Christian criticism. In Christ and in his "life for others," the essential structures of all life are revealed. Contemporary art forms do not see the reality of life in these terms. Christians must enter the contest and say with compassion and with a complete sense of stand-

[52]William F. Lynch, S. J., *Christ and Apollo: The Dimensions of the Literary Imagination* (New York: Sheed and Ward, 1960).

[53]TeSelle, *Literature and the Christian Life,* p. 53.

[54]John David Maguire, *The Dance of the Pilgrim* (New York: The Association Press, 1967), pp. 9-123.

[55]Chad Walsh, "A Hope for Literature" in *The Climate of Faith in Modern Literature* (New York: Seabury Press, 1964), pp. 223-233.

[56]Edmund Fuller, *Man in Modern Fiction* (New York: Vintage Books, 1958), pp. 3-19.

ing alongside that the Christian word about life is both real and possible and constitutes the fulfilling pattern.[57]

For Sallie TeSelle, Christian aesthetics should see its role in relation to the arts in terms of hints and insights rather than directives and a full-blown theory of art.[58] Well-known theological critic Tom Driver seeks to remind his fellow theologians that contemporary artists largely reflect the contemporary world with honesty and sensitivity. The artists are the products of a culture as much as its creators. It is important to note whether or not an artist handles language well, has the power of description and sustained imagery, and displays form and consistency. There should be a careful discrimination between authentic writers and cheap "muckrakers." These warnings need to be kept in mind before the critic rushes on to moral judgments. And at the base of prophetic judgment should be love.[59]

Amos Wilder points out that the theologian-critic often makes the mistake, also found in other critics, of violating proper method by a prior dogmatic. The theologian should admit that each art has its own refined disciplines, whose independence should be guarded. He should also admit that artistic criticism has its own sophisticated and scrupulous procedures. But such rightful autonomy does not mean that there are not ultimate issues at stake. Ultimate visions can and should be judged by theological criteria. If he is not careful, the theologian can show too much breadth and tolerance. If he succumbs to either temptation, dogmatism, or lack of conviction, profitable dialogue is frustrated. The floods of art forms call for Christian discrimination at every level.[60]

A vigorous theological critic, John Killinger, suggests that it is a theologian's solemn task to interpret and editorialize. Killinger grants the diagnostic, therapeutic, and even salutary virtues of many art forms. He allows them their integrity and

---

[57]Nathan A. Scott, Jr., "Faith and Art in a World Awry" in *The Climate of Faith in Modern Literature* (New York: Seabury Press, 1964), pp. 223-233.

[58]TeSelle, *Literature and the Christian Life*, pp. 36-39.

[59]Tom F. Driver, "Literary Criticism and the Christian Conscience," *Christianity and Crisis*, (July 7, 1957), pp. 91-94.

[60]Wilder, *The New Voice*, pp. 25f.

independence as art forms. Nevertheless, the theologian cannot resign his critical function and remain Christian. He must judge on the basis of theological criteria.[61]

Appreciation is always in order for artists who represent the essential mood of the Christian faith. Recognition should be given to those artists who borrow from the Christian structure. But these emphases are not basic enough. Evaluation must be made from the standpoint of the fundamental concepts of the biblical world-view. Examples of such evaluation as applied to contemporary literature, drama, and painting and, to a lesser extent, to other art forms will be given in the following chapters.

Let us assume that the theologian has set forth the fundamental concepts of the biblical world-view and has compared them with the poetic visions or world-views of representative art forms. What next? What criteria might be accepted on the open market? Generally accepted criteria include comprehensiveness, coherence, and creativity. Which view humanizes instead of dehumanizing? Which view can give the fullest account of reality in all of its aspects and meet man's deepest problems most adequately?

But perhaps the most needed approach in our time is not just in terms of *thinking,* but also in terms of *being* and in terms of a new *style* of life. Which view, when "fleshed out," will be found most appealing? Christ, in the days of his flesh, was not afraid of such a challenge. Who can forget his haunting words, "And I, if I be lifted up, will draw all men unto me."[62]

---

[61]John Killinger, *The Failure of Theology in Modern Literature* (New York: Abingdon Press, 1963), pp. 11-37.

[62]Hendrik Kraemer, *World Cultures and World Religions* (Philadelphia: The Westminster Press, 1960), p. 376. Cf. also John 12:32.

II

THEOLOGY AND CONTEMPORARY LITERATURE

Introduction

FOR ROGER HAZELTON, the work of the Christian theologian is analogous to the alternate expansions and contractions of the heart. There are times when the Christian faith has to turn inward upon itself toward self-discovery and self-definition. But then there are other times when it is important that it move out into the world again on the basis of this self-understanding. In this outward movement it must seek out and come to grips with areas from which earlier it had strategically withdrawn.[1]

Is it not true that we are now moving as theologians, professional and lay, into this second phase? And literature and drama vividly and powerfully represent the realities which constitute our world environment! In some cases the artist consciously expresses in fresh and vivid imagery basic Christian themes. More often, in our times, he presents visions

---

[1] Roger Hazelton, *New Accents in Contemporary Theology* (New York: Harper and Bros., 1960), pp. 11f.

which are partial, one-sided, and negative. The contemporary literary artist's root metaphors are quite often the death of God, the frontier, the boundary situation, shipwreck, the void, abyss, desert ruins, nightmare, estrangement, flight, and nausea.[2] In any case, the theologian will find the conversation challenging and provocative if not optimistic. In addition, as was seen in chapter one, it is the theologian's responsibility to evaluate literary and dramatic visions by the revealed model which finds the center, norm, and power for existence in Jesus Christ.

Literature and drama can be classified as negative, indirectly religious, and directly religious. Each of these three types deserves detailed treatment.[3] It would seem, however, that the most urgent task of our time is to develop a response to the powerful contemporary artistic movements which deny the fundamental Christian affirmations.[4]

Karl Mannheim contends that the whole drive of our positivistic culture has encouraged the belief that all experiences are of equal importance. This view tends to attribute radical significance to nothing. The great primordial images and guiding principles have been neutralized.[5] The majority of artists have found no radical organizing principles with which to work. Thus, the artist is driven into the corridors of his own private experience to try to construct some viable system of belief for himself. He has descended into his own mind to search for a clue by which the anarchy of experience might be

---

[2]William V. Spanos, "The Critical Imperatives of Alienation: The Theological Perspective of Nathan Scott's Literary Criticism" in *The Journal of Religion,* XLVII (January, 1968), p. 92.

[3]For a more detailed treatment of all three types see Newport, "Questions Ministers Ask About Contemporary Literature and Drama," pp. 31-47.

[4]The titles of several significant studies in the theology-literature conversation bear out the prevalence of the negative emphasis. Cf. Anthony T. Padovano, *The Estranged God: Modern Man's Search for Belief,* Modern Theology Library (New York: Sheed and Ward, 1966); Cleanth Brooks, *The Hidden God: Studies in Hemingway, Faulkner, Yeats, Eliot, and Warren* (New Haven: Yale University Press, 1963); Harry J. Mooney, Jr., and Thomas F. Staley, eds., *The Shapeless Gods* (Pittsburgh: University of Pittsburgh Press, 1968); and Gabriel Vahanian, *Wait Without Idols* (New York: George Braziller, 1964).

[5]Karl Mannheim, *Diagnosis of Our Time* (New York: Oxford, 1944), pp. 146-148.

given shape and significance. He has had to become, in a sense, his own guide.[6] This helps to account for the obscurity of a modern artist such as James Joyce.

What are the implications of the nightmare world of Kafka, the tragic probings of Camus, and the amorality of the Theater of the Absurd? This is more urgent for the contemporary theologian than discussing the better-charted areas of the Classical world-view and its literary and dramatic expression.[7]

In the next two chapters, therefore, attention will be given to representative literature and drama and other art forms of intellectual and artistic value which can be called "negative." "Negative" implies that the works under consideration do not consciously reflect Christian values and concepts for the sake of a Christian presentation. Negative literature and drama will be considered under the headings of Classical-Modern and Post-Modern.

Classical-Modern Literature

Renaissance man, typified by Leonardo da Vinci, sought a humanistic unity. Reformation man found unity in biblical revelation.[8] The great Classical-Moderns in literature—Camus, Hemingway, Faulkner, and Kafka—report the fundamental human reality as that of disruption and anxiety, nostalgia and loneliness. Even though it is primarily negative, this literature has depth and meaning. In many cases, it has clarity of form and often quickens in us the sensation of beauty. It engages in a polemic with the world of good. Thus, it is called Classical-Modern.[9]

The collapse, first in Western Europe and then later in the United States, of the traditional acceptance of the Judaeo-Christian system of referents and sanctions led to the emerg-

---

[6]Scott, *Broken Center,* p. 8.

[7]W. Moelwyn Merchant, *Creed and Drama* (Philadelphia: Fortress Press, 1965), pp. 113-115.

[8]Francis A. Schaeffer, *Escape From Reason* (Chicago: Inter-Varsity Press, 1968), p. 50.

[9]Nathan A. Scott, Jr., *Negative Capability* (New Haven: Yale University Press, 1969), pp. 7f.

ence of radical alienation as the life style of many modern men. As has been noted, this development has driven the artist out of the precincts of relative certainty.[10] The Classical-Moderns, largely rejecting older referents and metaphysics, have undertaken to find a stay against the confusion of the world with new myths. They offer us vast metaphors and parables about time, history, and the human prospect. In their own inverted way, they seek to give order and form to the formlessness of modern reality.[11] The Classical-Moderns seem to sense that almost the whole job of culture has been dumped in the artist's hands.[12]

Theology has been greatly quickened by the Classical-Moderns. Although they are secular and usually do not use traditional Christian frames, they do focus on ultimate issues. They have improvised into existence new systems of meaning and faith, and in inverted ways they are concerned with the whole issue of salvation.

The literary artists chosen as representatives of the Classical-Moderns are Camus, Hemingway, Faulkner, and Kafka. Kafka is considered as a transitional figure between the Classical-Moderns and the Post-Modern phase of literature.

ALBERT CAMUS

Perhaps the most important of the Classical-Moderns in literature is the French literary artist, Camus. He is probably the most widely read and attractive negative witness the twentieth century has produced. Henri Peyre of Yale states that no French novel of the present century has been submitted to so many exegetical analyses in America as has *The Stranger*.[13]

---

[10]Spanos, "Critical Imperatives," p. 90. Cf. also Jean-Paul Sartre, *What is Literature?* trans. by Bernard Frechtman (New York: Harper and Row, 1965) for the first statement of this idea.

[11]Scott, *Negative Capability,* p. 31.

[12]R. P. Blackmur, *The Lion and the Honeycomb,* Harvest Books (New York: Harcourt, Brace and World, 1955), p. 206.

[13]Henri Peyre, *Modern Literature: The Literature of France* (Englewood Cliffs, N. J.: Prentice-Hall, Inc., 1966), p. 196. Cf. Germaine Bree, *Camus* (New Brunswick, N. J.: Rutgers University Press, 1959) for details of his life.

Although Camus only produced five major works, the quality of his writing was recognized by the Nobel Prize award in 1957. His tragic death in a car accident occurred in 1960 at the age of forty-seven. In fact, his whole life tended towards tragedy. He was born in war-torn Algeria of a mother who could neither read nor write. She also had a speech defect and was deaf. His father was killed in World War I, leaving his mother with two small sons, and he was forced from home during the Second World War by German occupation. He was harassed by tuberculosis.

The world-view of Camus is structured around two fundamental concepts: the Absurd and Rebellion.

The *Myth of Sisyphus* presents the notion of an individual before a fragmented and absurd universe. *The Stranger* brings the absurd to one's emotions.

Absurdity, however, is not the final word for Camus. It is only the environment for Rebellion. In *The Rebel,* life is affirmed as good, but we struggle without hope. Metaphysical rebellion means that man protests his condition. In *The Plague,* man is called to a rebellion against suffering and against the separation of man from man. There is value in solidarity in rebellion.

In *The Fall,* Camus speaks of a man in tension before himself. Tension, guilt, and exile come not from the outside but from inside a man's heart.

For Camus, this world is the only truth we have. Until we find further answers, we must live in solidarity, struggle, and guilt.[14] Although Camus dealt with philosophical problems, his was primarily a concrete and emotional response to life.

Camus is an excellent example of a Classical-Modern. Although he did not accept the Christian view, he did accept responsibility and had deep concern for man's plight. He helped in the French Resistance. Camus called for a positive reaction to the absurdity of life, even though he offered no meaning for life beyond rebellion. In his own way, he did try to offer a model for life.

---

[14]Anthony T. Padovano, *The Estranged God* (New York: Sheed and Ward, 1966), pp. 101-132.

ERNEST HEMINGWAY

A second Classical-Modern is the American novelist, Ernest Hemingway. Unlike Camus, Hemingway was born into a middle-class, Protestant, provincial home. He reacted to middle-class mid-America, leaving his background to seek adventure, violence, and women. Hemingway reports that just to be in this world is to be confronted with evil, suffering, chaos, futility, and death. The universe is cold and empty. The idea of God is not compatible with this kind of world. *The Sun Also Rises* and *A Farewell to Arms* portray this harsh world.

Even more negative is the concept of "nothingness" which is vividly described in his short story entitled "A Clean, Well-Lighted Place." The older waiter in this terse, vivid story reflects on the sense of "nothingness" or "nada" that characterizes his life. He paraphrases the Lord's Prayer by saying: "Our nada who art in nada, nada be thy name." In *A Farewell to Arms* this "nothingness" is portrayed in the form of darkness.

The "nothingness" which overcomes Frederick and Catherine in *A Farewell to Arms* is less harsh with Santiago in *The Old Man and the Sea*. *The Sun Also Rises* is a story of a man lost in a world where God does not exist and where each must create his own rules for life. Rain becomes a symbol of all-pervasive evil. Alienation is portrayed by showing Frederick and Catherine as expatriates, unmarried, refugees from the war, without religious faith. Even human love does not provide a final or ultimate answer for Frederick and Catherine.[15]

Ritual is Hemingway's requirement to impose meaning on the nothingness which overcomes us in death, or sooner if we live as cowards. This ritual is religious in essence. It is pure and non-pragmatic. The bullfighter, for example, must kill cleanly, in exquisite form, with no malice or fear. Robert Jordan, in *For Whom the Bell Tolls,* shows duty and honor as part of the Hemingway code. The spiritual dimensions of hu-

---

[15]Anthony T. Padovano, *American Culture and the Quest for Christ* (New York: Sheed and Ward, 1970), pp. 176-190. For details on the life and career of Hemingway see the definitive bibliography by Carlos Baker, *Ernest Hemingway, A Life Story* (New York: Charles Scribner's Sons, 1969).

man victory are most graphically portrayed in *The Old Man and the Sea*. Santiago, as an old man, has little physical strength for the ritualized struggle with the great fish. He does have spiritual resources, and he relies on these for the final conflict of his life. There are obvious Christological references. Hemingway said to his lost generation that we can seize a momentary, ritualized meaning in grace under pressure from a cold, empty universe. We have no God but we are to be men to the end. Although Hemingway never formally accepted Christianity, in his search for meaning he affirmed its residual forms and fundamental themes.[16]

Hemingway is a Voluntarist and suffered from the pessimism which is typical of Voluntarists from Schopenhauer to Freud. In place of happiness and spiritual experiences, there is discipline and action. Action becomes an escape from "nada" or nothingness. In *For Whom the Bell Tolls,* Robert Jordan acts as a man who fulfills his mission and dies.[17]

Hemingway, unfortunately, limits his concern with salvation to individualism. Each man faces his moment alone. Enlightenment is only for the elite. The curious tourists know little of the ritual, suffering, and gallantry of Santiago's struggle with the fish in *The Old Man and the Sea.*[18]

Unlike Camus, Hemingway fails to recognize the evil within man. His humanistic resources were limited, as can be seen in his own tragic death. But he is a Classical-Modernist. In an unforgettable style, he does offer a positive way, limited as it may be, to face the evil, suffering, and chaos of life.

WILLIAM FAULKNER

The *London Times* called the third Classical-Modern, William Faulkner, the watershed writer in the history.of Ameri-

---

[16]Ibid, pp. 174-190.
[17]Ibid., pp. 176-183.
[18]Ibid., pp. 177f. Cf. also Cleanth Brooks, *The Hidden God: Studies in Hemingway, Faulkner, Yeats, Eliot and Warren* (New Haven: Yale University Press, 1964), p. 14. Cf. also Robert P. Weeks, ed., *Hemingway: A Collection of Critical Essays* (Englewood Cliffs, N. J.: Prentice-Hall, Inc., 1962).

can literature. Before his death, Camus spoke of Faulkner as the greatest living creator of fiction. Faulkner may well be the most profound and the most religious writer our culture has produced. On the surface, he seems to be a writer whose work is a poetic elaboration of the "legend" of the South. Beneath the surface he raises basic questions about virtue, evil, the overcoming of the betrayal of our past, and how to learn compassion in deprivation and suffering.[19]

Faulkner's writings are dominated by an awareness of guilt. This guilt arises both from personal evil and complicity in human history. Along with Ingmar Bergman, Faulkner believes in original sin more passionately than he believes in divine love.

Sanctuary and *Absalom, Absalom!* deal with sexual and racial violation and subsequent destruction. *Light in August* is more than a novel of racial identification. It is a novel of self-estrangement. It accepts original sin. Joe Christmas, like Christ, dies not only because of the resistance of his contemporaries, but because of earlier deeds from which men continue to suffer because they have a common history.

In spite of the power of evil, there is more than total darkness in Faulkner's world. Sometimes this hope is set in a Christological framework as in *As I Lay Dying, A Fable,* and *The Sound and the Fury. The Bear* is also hopeful. It considers the possibility of a transcendent revelation or vision for those who sensitize themselves to the mystical and spiritual realities of life.[20]

The most important of the works of this Nobel and Pulitzer Prize winner is *The Sound and the Fury.* Faulkner saw the Oxford, Mississippi, area, which he called Yoknapatawpha County, as the microcosm of all mankind. In a cumbersome, complicated, elaborate, and rich style Faulkner exposes the social and psychological mechanisms which represent the destructive elements in society. He sounds a warning against social tyranny and fossilized religious sanctions. A novel of this

[19]Ibid., p. 219.
[20]Ibid., pp. 220-222, 243, 247, 258, 284.

type touches more profound levels than does a sociological analysis.[21]

As the title, taken from Shakespeare's *Macbeth* would suggest, *The Sound and the Fury* points to the meaninglessness of life. He tells the story in four different times and ways. First, it is told through the stream of consciousness of Benjy, the idiot. Man finds himself trapped in a meaningless maze of events much as did Benjy. In a second story, man tries to live beyond time, as did Quentin. But this only leads to destruction. In a third story, like Jason, man reduces time to the rational and mechanical. This ends in materialism.[22]

In a more positive manner than most of the Classical-Moderns, the fourth story from the perspective of the Negro slave, Dilsey, offers a transcendent vision. Some call this section of the novel an indirect instead of a negative witness. During the Easter Sunday sermon, Dilsey sees the beginning and the end. Man will not merely endure, but he will prevail. The vision of the Christian drama can give man power and an overarching perspective. There is a way out. In fact, Vahanian goes so far as to contend that the four sections in *The Sound and the Fury* listed above are the four moments of existence: innocence; the fall; paradise lost; and redemption.[23]

FRANZ KAFKA

The fourth representative, Franz Kafka, the European Jew, is a transitional figure in thought, if not in chronology (he died in 1924), between Classical-Moderns and Post-Moderns. As is true of the Post-Modern literary figures, there is less

[21]Amos N. Wilder, *Theology and Modern Literature* (Cambridge: Harvard University Press, 1967), p. 125.

[22]For discussions of Faulkner's view of time see Olga Vickery, *The Novels of William Faulkner* (Baton Rouge, La.: Louisiana State University Press, 1964); Margaret Church, *Time and Reality* (The University of North Carolina Press, 1949); John W. Hunt, *William Faulkner: Art in Theological Tension* (Syracuse University Press, 1965); and Cleanth Brooks, *William Faulkner: The Yoknapatawpha County* (New Haven: Yale University Press, 1963).

[23]Gabriel Vahanian, *Wait Without Idols* (New York: George Braziller, 1964), p. 95.

coherence and structure in his works than in the creations of most Classical-Moderns. His encounter with the world is ambiguous and radical. Kafka makes few attempts to subdue anarchy and hold together reality and justice. His is a tantalizing and opaque fiction whose meaning is deliberately left open and unresolved.[24]

Kafka's two greatest works are *The Trial* and *The Castle*. *The Trial* tells of man's frustrating pursuit of innocence and justice. Joseph K. is aware of guilt but sees no way out. He wants, but cannot find, both human and supra-human acceptance in a universe whose pattern and meaning are uncertain and unknowable.

In *The Castle,* man searches for a relationship with something durable, definite, and final but cannot find it. Man wants to know who he is, but he is finally alone.[25]

In John Bunyan's *Pilgrim's Progress,* Pilgrim reaches his goal. A clear-cut system was behind this allegory. Coming after Nietzsche, Kafka found no such system. Its absence characterizes his journey.[26]

Seldom in literature is absurdity expressed so vividly as in *The Trial*. Joseph K. is a good and efficient man yet he is arrested. The legal proceedings are nonsensical. In order to express absurdity Kafka oftentimes uses what are called grotesques.

Despite the emphasis on absurdity, Kafka is still a Classical-Modern, for he has man persisting in his hopeless struggle. He keeps on trying to reach the Castle. Man continues to attempt to become a respected citizen in the novel *Amerika* despite failure after failure.[27]

The Trial and *The Castle*, both pivotal modernist novels,

---

[24]Scott, *Negative Capability*, p. 33.

[25]Padovano, *The Estranged God*, pp. 93-101.

[26]Stanley Romaine Hopper, "Literature—The Author in Search of His Anecdote," in *Restless Adventure*, ed. Roger L. Shinn (New York: Charles Scribner's Sons, 1968), p. 107.

[27]For helpful discussions on the background of Kafka see Harry Slochourer, *Literature and Philosophy Between Two World Wars* (New York: Citadel Press, 1964), pp. 103-125 and Louis R. Glessman and Eugene Feldman, eds., *The Worlds of Kafka and Cuevas* (Philadelphia: Falcon Press, 1959).

are forerunners of two distinct forms that have taken shape in the American novel: the absurdist and the activist. As has been noted, *The Trial* is absurd in many ways. *The Castle* has an activist hero, alienated it is true, but at the same time one who seeks for himself an improbable but transcendent self. Not that he obtains his goal (he does not). He does, however, explore the possibles beyond the givens and beyond the probable. K., in *The Castle,* is a germinal presentation of this activist hero.[28]

In this activist mode have come a number of American novelists such as Saul Bellow, J. D. Salinger, Norman Mailer, Bernard Malamud, Herbert Gold, and Philip Roth. The Negro activists include James Baldwin and Ralph Ellison. Other writers with activist tendencies include William Styron and R. V. Cassill.[29]

Here is the negative witness. Kafka has a vivid recognition of alienation as the peculiar form of suffering for contemporary man. Man is seen as helpless and guilty. It is a literary portrayal of the philosophical thought of Nietzsche.

Other important negative literary witnesses can also be designated as Classical-Moderns. Thomas Wolfe portrays loneliness and the tragic grandeur of man in *Look Homeward, Angel* and in *You Can't Go Home Again.* In *Of Time and the River,* as well as other books, Wolfe is concerned about the limits of time. J. D. Salinger in *The Catcher in the Rye* and *Franny and Zooey* exposes "phoniness" in the older generation. He seeks sincerity, truth, and innocence which he cannot find in the adult world. William Golding's *Lord of the Flies* discounts man's innocence and vividly describes the evil of man brought on by his selfishness and greed. *Free Fall* and *The Spire* continue William Golding's exploration of the nature of man. In *Barabbas,* Par Lagerkvist portrays in an unforgettable way the difficulty of belief in our time. George Orwell also has a negative commentary on modern man. The world of the novel *1984* is a world of hate.[30]

---

[28]Helen Weinberg, *The New Novel in America* (Ithaca, N. Y.: Cornell University Press), pp. 10-13.
[29]Ibid., pp. 165, 186.
[30]Padovano, *The Estranged God,* p. 154.

Post-Modern Developments in Non-literary Arts

The Post-Modern scene in literature is strikingly different. Little attempt is made by this literature to clarify or transfigure the human reality. The novels are non-narrative. They make no attempt to give any shape to the immense panorama of anarchy which is our world. Post-Modern writings are fragmentary. They do little more than illustrate the world's opaque mysteriousness and contingency. This literature has little depth and tends towards displeasure. Susan Sontag calls it the "new sensibility." This "new sensibility" is a tendency governing the central movement in the artistic culture of the present time. It applies to painting, architecture, and movies as well as literature and drama.[31] In order to better understand developments in Post-Modern literature, parallel developments in painting, music, architecture, movies, and philosophy will be surveyed briefly.

PAINTING

The Post-Modern sensibility or style can be seen clearly in the new painting. A painting in the new style does not "mean" anything extrinsic to itself. It is simply so much paint on a certain area of canvas. The paintings of Kenneth Noland, Franz Kline, Mark Rothko, and Frank Stella afford no chance to enjoy the convergences of perspective, spatial intervals, linear rhythms, and orchestrations of plane and volume found in Classical-Moderns. This latter group of painters would include Cézanne, Matisse, Chagall, and Picasso. Franz Kline, for example, wants his canvases to be simply large white fields bearing broad strokes of black.[32]

MUSIC

The avant-garde in music has as its chief American spokesman, John Cage. Cage calls for an elimination of

[31]Scott, *Negative Capability*, pp. 22-32, 60.
[32]Ibid., pp. 11, 19, 20. Cf. Chapter IV for a fuller and more qualified discussion. Excellent resumes found in Neville Weston, *Kaleidoscope of Modern Art* (London: George C. Harrap and Co., 1968).

human sentiments and the patterns of human feelings. A musical composition will simply present sounds in the sheer "thereness" of their acousticality. There should be an avoidance of a rhythmically ordered climax or sequence. Sound is to be objective and anonymous and contain no depth.[33]

As can be seen, Cage has set himself against the whole Western tradition of musical composition. For Cage, too many people do not listen for the sound of music but try to listen *through* the sound to the intention of the composer. Sound, such as doorbells and car engines, has a value and a fascination in its own right which must be liberated. The composers must present the sound as sound and not as the medium for an idea. In order to accomplish this, Cage demolishes patterns, melody, and themes, often scoring his music in sequences determined by the toss of a coin. The past is an oppressor in music.[34]

Cage's emphasis on what *is* is akin to the "now" experience emphasis of youth culture. It seems to lack interest in hoping, creating, or changing. There is the danger of slipshod techniques and little interest in disciplined change.[35]

ARCHITECTURE

This depthlessness is also a striking feature of the Post-Modern architecture. A public building is not visibly in any way to be a celebration of our common humanity. It is simply a structure of concrete or steel. Mies von der Rohe, an exemplar, wants his Chicago apartment-skyscrapers to be simply skeletons of steel and glass—nothing more, only the sheer thereness of the raw materials in their unhumanized facticity.[36]

MOVIES

Even the movies have gone Post-Modern. For the avant-

---

[33]Ibid., p. 9. Cf. also Elliot Schwartz and Barney Childs, *Contemporary Composers on Contemporary Music* (New York: Holt, Rinehart and Winston, 1967), and John Cage, *Silence* (Cambridge, Mass: MIT Press, 1967).
[34]Cox, *Feast of Fools*, pp. 37-39.
[35]Ibid., p. 41.
[36]Scott, *Negative Capability*, pp. 10f.

garde, the film no longer has as its ideal the documentary, as an eyewitness record of verifiable reality. The directors have become artists and have largely replaced the "star" system. The director is seen as the primary cause and author in every phase of the total sequence. He uses his work to express a personal vision of the world. "Stories" are secondary to the moments of revelation created by sound or photography or editing. The traditional linear plot is secondary to the manipulation of the forms and movements of screen images. The radical present replaces the continuity of concrete, objective time. This effect is produced by splicing scenes without connections. The scenes are oftentimes unexpected, contradictory, and seemingly irrelevant.[37]

A personal experience on a first viewing of Fellini's *8½* and *Juliet of the Spirits* confirmed the differences between Post-Modern films and the Classical-Moderns of William Wyler, George Stevens, John Huston, and Rossellini. No categories will apply to *Juliet of the Spirits*. One does not know if it is real, illusory, psychological, or insanity. It is a tyranny of the visual, of the image for its own sake. In *The Satyricon,* Fellini has no rising curve toward climactic action and denouement. There is little linear progression. Rather, he has allowed the film to flow from incident to incident, so that when we view it we see it as a dream, perhaps a nightmare of ancient Rome.[38]

Bergman's *Silence* harries the viewer with images of vacuity, ambiguity, and perplexity. It is unrelated, having little meaning. *Through a Glass Darkly* portrays a few isolated people cut off from everything. The mood of *Winter Light* is cold and lonely. In *The Silence* Bergman's leading characters are in a foreign land, in a deserted hotel, unable to communicate with each other or anyone else. It is a portrayal of man's need of communication and love. In these three films, the protag-

---

[37]Ibid., pp. 12-14. For film in general see Harris Dienstrfrey, "The New American Film" in *The New American Arts,* ed. Richard Kostelanetz (New York: Collier Books, 1965), pp. 31-39, and Gregory Battcock, *The New American Cinema* (New York: E. P. Dutton Co., 1966), and "The Film Maker as Ascendant Star" in *Time* (July 4, 1969), pp. 46-51.

[38]Hollis Alpert, "The Fellinicon," in *Saturday Review* (March 14, 1970), pp. 42-44.

onists cannot get hold of God, so they destroy themselves in madness, despair over their inability to love, or move inexorably toward physical and spiritual death.[39]

Godard's *Weekend* strings together the grotesque and fragmented, and the sequence of events becomes more random as the film concludes. *Weekend* makes little distinction between illusion and reality. In *One American Movie,* Godard uses a free-form polemic set in a Brooklyn ghetto to paint a pessimistic picture of the United States.

Antonioni's *Blow-Up* is also random including a game of non-tennis with no rackets, net, or ball. The hero concludes that there is no use to distinguish reality from illusion.[40] There is a relationship between a film such as Antonioni's *L'Avventura* and the novels of James Joyce. The series of images flashing on the screen is ordered not by space and time, as we commonly know them, but by a space and time created by the mind. In *L'Avventura,* the symbol of human alienation and loneliness comes not through a verbal image but through twenty-five minutes of pictures of people in lonely situations.[41]

An extreme example of the Post-Modern film is Alain Resnais' *The Last Year at Marienbad.* The scenario was written by a prominent Post-Modern novelist, Alain Robbe-Grillet. It is a radical exemplification of the new period-style. The setting is a vast baroque hotel with long, endless corridors. Three personages, designated as A, a woman, and two men, X and M, are seen in conversation. In the midst of their strange discussions, the camera roams over the details of the hotel and grounds in a wild and grotesque way. Strange sounds and dazzling white effects are plentiful. It is a camera show, a director's show, and has little to do with the characters.

[39]William Hamilton, "Bergman and Polanski on the Death of God" in John C. Cooper and Carl Skrade, *Celluloid and Symbols* (Philadelphia: Fortress Press, 1970), pp. 62, 71, 87.

[40]Scott, *Negative Capability,* pp. 18-20. Additional material on film is found in *Drum* (Philadelphia: J. B. Lippincott Co., 1969), p. 106, and Jerry H. Gill, *Ingmar Bergman and the Search for Meaning* (Grand Rapids: W. B. Eerdmans Co., 1969) and Andrew Sarris (ed.), *Interviews with Film Directors* (New York: Avon Books, 1967) and Arthur Gibson, *The Silence of God* (New York: Harper and Co., 1969).

[41]Marian C. Sheridan, et al., *The Motion Picture and the Teaching of English* (New York: Appleton-Century-Crofts, 1965), pp. 45, 134.

It is not "about" anything at all. It is an art object to present the immediacy of film images.[42]

In *The Last Year at Marienbad,* according to Morrissette, we enter into a fictional realm of externalized imagination. There are inner duplications and chronological deformations. The film is more than the simple objectification of mental content. It creates new patterns of aesthetic reality.[43] It does demonstrate, however, to Robbe-Grillet's satisfaction, that the only way to approach concepts is through physical objects and not, as most people would say, through consciousness. Consciousness for Robbe-Grillet is a highly suspect construction upon the sensible world. Memory and imagination are firmly dependent on the physical. Memories depend on objects. He calls for a return to the centrality of the physical as the only true reality. Character is defended in terms of sense experience.[44]

PHILOSOPHY

There is even a Post-Modern emphasis in philosophy— British linguistic philosophy. The "early" Wittgenstein, a leader of the movement, was concerned with the definition of words. From this perspective, philosophy should primarily be a "critique of language" or "the logical clarification of thoughts." Since you can't speak of God and ultimate questions in an empirical or logical way—be silent! Driven out of many philosophy classrooms, living philosophical discussion has moved into unusual settings—such as philosophic astronomy, modern jazz, or among the real hippies.[45] To fill up the intellectual vacuum, many people turn to drugs, Zen, Hindu Mysticism, or Esalen in seeking a vision or mystical experience.

---

[42]Scott, *Negative Capability,* pp. 16,24, cf. also Francis A. Schaeffer, *Escape From Reason* (Chicago: Inter-Varsity Press, 1968), p. 73 and John Ward, *Alain Resnais* (Garden City, N.Y.: Doubleday and Co., 1968), pp. 39-62. Alain Robbe-Grillet has produced a recent film *L'Immortelle* which embodies the same principles and approach.

[43]Bruce Morrissette, *Alain Robbe-Grillet* (New York: Columbia University Press, 1965), pp. 36f.

[44]Ward, *Alain Resnais,* pp. 43f., 56.

[45]Scott, *Negative Capability,* p. 19. Cf., also Schaeffer, *Escape From Reason,* pp. 50, 57.

These brief descriptions of the Post-Modern developments in painting, music, architecture, movies, and philosophy should help to prepare us to understand the avant-garde developments in literature and drama.

Post-Modern European Literature

Susan Sontag, among others, affirms that the classical tradition is tired and somewhat exhausted. The classical tradition assumes that prose fiction is to render a world in terms of a credible story, peopled with complex characters. The narrative is to be linear in construction and the writing is to be ordinary discursive writing. The novel is not so much a work of art as a mirror of reality. It is to dramatize issues and supply information. There is evidence of a new Post-Modern, non-classical tradition developing in literature.[46]

The beginnings of an Anglo-American avant-garde tradition existed in the work of James Joyce, Virginia Woolf, Samuel Beckett, Gertrude Stein, Nathanael West, and John Dos Passos. These writers began to be concerned with form, with literature as works of art, as aesthetic objects, and not just as representations of outer reality. This tendency toward form is more advanced in representational art forms such as dance, painting, and sculpture. Joyce in *Ulysses* was a pioneer in this regard in the novel. One direction for literature would be to discard the traditional supremacy of the "story" or "plot." A rather new form of order proceeds by the cultivation of chance or casual means of composition. An example of this type of development is William S. Burroughs in *The Soft Machine* and *Naked Lunch*. He uses a "collage technique." Joyce was concerned with the texture (density, richness, poetry) of language as the vehicle of narrative. Peter Weiss has revived the "use" of insanity in *Marat/Sade*.[47]

---

[46]Susan Sontag, "Literature," *The Great Ideas Today 1966*, eds. R. M. Hutchins and M. J. Adler (Chicago: Encyclopedia Britannica, Inc., 1966), pp. 154f., 159f., 165, 170, 180.
[47]Ibid., pp. 160-162, 165, 170, 180.

ALAIN ROBBE-GRILLET

The chief contemporary theorist of Post-Modern literature is the French writer, Alain Robbe-Grillet. His major concern is with the novel. According to Robbe-Grillet, the novel must be liberated from the tradition of "psychological analysis." The answer is found in purging literature of old structures of plot and character and of the old eloquence. Just describe things that are there. Do away with the omnipotence of the person and the old cult of the human.[48]

Robbe-Grillet's essays in *For a New Novel* are an attempt to formulate a new aesthetic for prose literature. He is the author of four major novels: *The Erasers, Le Voyeur, La Jalousie,* and *In the Labyrinth.* Robbe-Grillet speaks out against lifelikeness and psychologically credible characters. He calls for the writing of novels with a radical emphasis on the most objective of the senses, sight, and a refusal of metaphor and analogy. Literature should point to nothing beyond what is described, nothing of a message. There should be an absorption of elements and devices which are parascientific and paratechnological. Literature should not shrink to mere self-conscious play and diversion.[49]

Bruce Morrissette disagrees with Roland Barthes that the main or only importance of Robbe-Grillet's work is its use of descriptions of *things.* For Morrissette there is more than a description of neutral "surfaces," devoid of depth. Rather Robbe-Grillet also creates levels of meanings, devises plots (of a different type), uses psychology, and does employ things in a referential manner. Robbe-Grillet's form involves social arrangements, interior duplications of themes and characters, and restructured chronology.[50]

As we have seen, the new movies have turned away from the universe of the human to a signification of the sheer *thereness* of familiar objects. According to Robbe-Grillet, this

---

[48]Scott, *Negative Capability,* pp. 10, 35. Cf. also Morrissette, *Alain Robbe-Grillet* and Scott, *Craters of the Spirit,* p. 170.

[49]Sontag, "Literature," pp. 184-186, 189.

[50]Morrissette, *Alain Robbe-Grillet, pp.* 5,7,8.

should be a model for the novel. A writer should exhibit the world in brute givenness apart from order. Concentrate on angles, planes, and surfaces.[51]

Robbe-Grillet, in two of his novels, *Le Voyeur* and *La Jalousie,* avoids creating characters and telling stories. He focuses attention upon the external world. There is little room for man. Most of the room is taken up by the hard, resistant materialities with which the ghostly remnants of men collide. In *La Jalousie* there is not a single reference to "I" or "me." In *Le Voyeur,* as the ship docks, page after page describes the details of the pier. He has no interest in the feelings, thoughts, or inwardness of his characters. Rather, he spends his time describing the strange opaqueness and density of the world's surfaces. The only thing true about the human presence is its "thereness."[52]

And so, with the extrusion of both characters and stories, Robbe-Grillet intends to stick to zero. The novelist is to convert the world and the reality of man into a kink of frozen, still-life. Very little can be said about them. No judgment is to be made. They are simply to be looked at with unprejudiced eyes.[53]

NATHALIE SARRAUTE

Nathalie Sarraute, another French writer and author of *Les Fruits d'or,* has a similar perspective. In *The Age of Suspicion,* she also pleads for a new departure. She states that we have now entered upon the age of suspicion. The reader is skeptical when the writer attempts to offer him anything more than simple reports on matters of fact. The literary medium should not be used as a vehicle of Reality or Myth. Instead, the literary enterprise should be confined to facts, little facts. For Nathalie Sarraute, that is all that counts. She wants to move away from characters, realism, and social and metaphysical concerns in the novel. Michel Butor, the author of *L'Emploi du Temps* and *Degres,* and Claude Simon, author of

---

[51]Scott, *Craters of the Spirit,* p. 171. Cf. also Alain Robbe-Grillet, *For a New Novel* (New York: Grove Press, 1965), p. 19.
[52]Ibid., pp. 171-174.
[53]Ibid., pp. 173, 174.

Le Palace and *La Route des Flanders,* represent a slightly different but similar perspective.[54]

For good or bad, the Post-Moderns in literature have been welcomed in the literary world, especially in the United States. Henri Peyre, formerly of France, and now professor of French at Yale University, is slightly amused at the way in which the scholars and teachers of the United States have pored over every word of the "new" French novelists. He reminds us that Robbe-Grillet came to literature from a career as an agricultural expert on exotic fruits and Claude Simon was previously a wine maker. The passionate interest of Americans for what is new amuses the more cynical Frenchmen. Peyre thinks that Americans should look at Robbe-Grillet with a little more humorous detachment after hearing this agronomist turned novelist claim as his precursors such men as Proust, Kafka, Joyce, and Faulkner.[55]

The veteran Francois Mauriac vigorously criticizes the Post-Moderns of France. He contends that all does not constantly slip down the drain to nothingness in a human being. Others have called the French Post-Modern writing the literature of boredom.[56]

Post-Modern American Literature

In the United States, there is a movement in Post-Modern literature generally parallel to the Continental avant-garde. Its definition is not as sharp, but there is the same general tendency at work in this country. It has some relationship to "black humor," and it utilizes a combination of tragic and comic modalities. There is a tendency toward abolishing formalizing structures. Discontinuity and lack of connection are noticeable in this literature. It emphasizes improvisation and unusual combinations of the farcical and horrific, and the

---

[54]Nathalie Sarraute, *The Age of Suspicion: Essays on the Novel,* trans. by Maria Jelas (New York: George Braziller, 1963), p. 57. Cf. also Scott, *Craters of the Spirit,* p. 174 and Ruth Z. Temple, *Nathalie Sarraute* (New York: Columbia University Press, 1968).
[55]Peyre, *Modern Literature,* pp. 198f.
[56]Ibid., p. 202.

bitter with the sweet.[57] The American Post-Moderns reject the Classical-Moderns, whom they say tend to be destiny moulders and imposers-upon. Nihilistic rather than humanistic impulses predominate. For these writers there is a disparity between hope and fact.[58]

Many of the American novels which have absurdist tendencies are still realistic in style: Bellow's *The Victim,* Friedman's *Stern,* Malamud's *The Assistant,* and Salinger's *The Catcher in the Rye* (in which the hero actively engages in the pursuit of a private truth but is at the same time the victim of the absurdity promulgated by the "sensible" world of adults). These novels have absurd tendencies and have at their center a passive, rationalistic, or hopelessly ineffectual victim-hero. He is usually dominated by his situation rather than creating or acting to change it. They have a more or less realistic surface with some surrealistic elements.[59]

Another group of American novels are absurdist with a stylized absurd surface. The absurd surface exaggerates. Through exaggeration and repetitions, grotesqueries, and unique, exotic, bizarre symbols, the absurdity found in life is transcribed through surreal descriptions. Special surrealistic situations are created to embody the inexplicable. Somewhat common situations, such as those of war, are exaggerated and distorted to produce a heightened effect of the sort experienced in dreams. Representative of the absurdist novels using surreal means to present the victim-hero's situation in addition to Joseph Heller's *Catch-22* and Pynchon's *V,* are Hawkes's *The Cannibal* and *Second Skin,* and John Barth's *The End of the Road* (and, to some extent, *The Sot-Weed Factor* and *Giles Goat-Boy,* although these seem more indebted to eighteenth-century satire).[60]

[57]Scott, *Negative Capability,* pp. 46f. Cf. also Richard Kostelanetz, "The New American Fiction," pp. 194-236 and Leonard Meyer, "The End of the Renaissance? Notes on the Radical Empiricism of the Avant-Garde," *The Hudson Review,* XVI (Summer, 1963), 169-86.

[58]John W. Hunt, "Comic Escape and Anti-Vision: The Novels of Joseph Heller and Thomas Pynchon" in *Adversity and Grace,* ed. Nathan A. Scott, Jr. (Chicago: The University of Chicago Press, 1968), pp. 91f.

[59]Weinberg, *The New Novel in America,* p. 10.

[60]Ibid., p. 11.

Representative men in the American Post-Modern group include Joseph Heller and Thomas Pynchon.

JOSEPH HELLER

A veteran of World War II, Joseph Heller has had a varied career as student (Fulbright scholar at Oxford), professor of English, and advertising writer for *Time* and *Look*. In addition to *Catch-22*, he wrote the motion picture script for Helen Gurley Brown's *Sex and the Single Girl*.

The initial response to Joseph Heller's *Catch-22* was extreme. Some called it an "emotional hodgepodge" and an outrage. Others refused to call it a book or a novel.[61] On the other hand, Nelson Algren calls it the best novel to come out of World War II or anywhere in years.[62] For those reared on Classical-Moderns it appeared too subtle in theme. These responses were anticipated by Heller. He contends that the critics were laughing at their own absurd world.[63]

Catch-22 is the story of John Yossarian, United States Air Force, a bombardier. Yossarian opposes his society and seeks ways to escape. The enemy for Yossarian is anybody who's going to get you killed, no matter *which* side he's on. In this novel, Heller uses fantasy, repetition, and reversal.

Yossarian couldn't be sent home on medical leave because of one catch and that was Catch-22. Catch-22 specified that a concern for one's safety in the face of dangers that were real and immediate was the process of a rational mind. If a man were crazy, he could be grounded. If he asked to be grounded, he was no longer crazy and would have to fly more missions. *Catch-22* is the phrase used for the paradox of evil.

The principle of Catch-22 centers around the idea that all coherence and rationality are frustrated. "How can he see he's got flies in his eyes if he's got flies in his eyes?" This

---

[61]R. G. Stern, "A Review of *Catch-22*," *New York Times Book Review*, (October 22, 1969), p. 50.
[62]Nelson Algren, "A Review of *Catch-22*," *Nation* (November 4, 1969), p. 193.
[63]Hunt, "Comic Escape and Anti-Vision," pp. 90-92. Cf. also Scott, *Negative Capability*, p. 47 and Joseph Heller, *Catch-22* (New York: Dell Publishing Co., 1961).

flippant paradox, says Yossarian, makes as much sense as anything else. He applies this sense of contradiction to the military and to business.[64]

Heller goes beyond Camus's and Sartre's concept of the "absurd." Instead of ending with absurdity, he begins with it. He seeks to assess human existence through the comic mode. For Heller, this is the only way in which life can have any meaning in a world of evil and death.

Absurdity underlies every dramatic incident in *Catch-22*. Heller seeks to keep the comic structure and yet project a bitter vision. The world is irrational and disconnected. It provides no basis for moral action. For Yossarian (and Heller) there is no God and therefore no eternity. There is only the existential space between the existential now and death, and everything conspires to shorten it—war, diseases, friends, enemies. At the end of the novel, Yossarian does try to make order out of chaos by going to Sweden—a symbol of Paradise.[65]

Although this zany novel outrages many who know from experience the ghastliness of war, through comic hyperbole Heller still finds a way to condemn what he thinks is the senselessness of war. Yossarian, though literally mad and quite paranoid by the end of the book, is shown by Heller to be the only sane man in it. In contrast to the ponderous logic of the generals and colonels around him, Yossarian's cowardice and craziness seem to be the only rational course. *Catch-22* is not just about war. Heller's vision is that there is an ultimate fraudulence and ridiculousness at the base of man's so-called rational society.[66]

In the midst of the difficulties of this era, it is not surprising that the comic structure should once again come to the forefront in literature. For the tragic approach, human finitude is a profound embarrassment and perhaps even a curse. The

[64]Ibid., pp. 94-98. Cf. also F. R. Karl, "Joseph Heller's *Catch-22:* Only Fools Walk in Darkness" in Harry T. Moore, ed., *Contemporary American Novelists* (Carbondale, Ill.: Southern Illinois University Press, 1966).
[65]Karl, "Joseph Heller's *Catch-22*," p. 138.
[66]Cox, *Feast of Fools*, p. 156.

comic approach reminds us of how deeply rooted we all are in the tangible things of the world. The comic asks us to accept our conditioned finitude.[67] The authentic Christian vision also stresses man's humanness and yet spares us from feeling that finitude is, of itself, an evil. The Christian is not inexorably doomed by his finitude. There is a way out.

THOMAS PYNCHON

Thomas Pynchon's prominent novels are *V* and *The Crying of Lot 49*. *V* won the prize for the best first novel of its year, 1963. These novels are quests for meaning but the author defeats his characters. They are comic novels of anti-vision. He is more openly interested in metaphysics than Heller, and yet more pessimistic.

In *V* three stories are told. Benny Profane's story is in the present tense. He is a constant "yo-yo'er" and has a meaningless quest in story one. In the second story, also in the present, Herbert Stencil quests for the meaning of the letter *V*, a reference to which he had found in his father's diary. In story three, which is over by 1942, Victoria Wren helps unravel the story of *V*. She seems to be part, at least, of what was denoted by the letter *"V."*

The images in *V* are violent. There are few coherent meanings. Victoria appears under a number of aliases and disguises: an English girl (Victoria), a saintly rat (Veronica), Botticelli's Venus, a German trollop (Vera), an Italian woman of wealth (Veronica), and, of course, the Virgin herself. Who is *V*? Pynchon does not give the answer.

Pynchon develops the theme of animation versus inanimation. *V*, as a paradigm of history, loses her identity and gradually becomes desexed. Victoria's personal progression toward inanimateness is portrayed by her bodily incorporating little bits of inert matter. These include a glass eye with a clock iris, a wig, false teeth, fabricated feet, and a star sapphire sewn into her navel. She becomes desexed and mech-

---

[67]Scott, *Broken Center,* pp. 91f., 103.

anized in all her functions including a digital machine in her skull.[68]

Though *V* is sometimes called "black-humor," it is one of the most intricate and elaborate novels of our time. Sklar states that it may be the first American novel of collage and abstract composition put together with parodies.[69] Gros says it is like listening to a scholarly but erratic documentation of hell.[70] Most will agree that Pynchon has imagination, audacity, philosophical and metaphysical sophistication.

For Pynchon, life is running down while it becomes mechanical and artificial. Life is made up of fragmentation and discontinuity. Asked what he has learned from all of his experiences, Benny replies that he hasn't learned a thing. But Benny and Stencil keep on questing. Like Heller, Pynchon's premise is absurdity. Unlike Heller, there is no call to freedom, but to an unblissful and tolerable ignorance threatened by the inanimate.[71]

The Crying of Lot 49 portrays the same anti-vision as *V*. Pynchon exposes the fragmentation of human experience.[72]

Both Heller and Pynchon have given us novels of absurdity. These novels are representative of the Post-Modern literature in the United States. Other prominent writers include John Barth, James Purdy, Richard Stern, and Bruce Friedman. John Barth, for example, in *The Sot-Weed Factor,* uses eight hundred and six pages to make a mockery of all written history—especially American history. History is seen as disordered. There are no first causes or definitive interpretations. Single events are absurd. Life as a whole resists any ordering interpretation. This is done in an eloquent style, funny, with striking phrases and a skillful use of parody. Barth's *The Floating Opera* is a parody of *The Myth of Sisyphus* by a Classical-Modernist, Camus. Theirs is an anti-teleological art

[68]Hunt, "Comic Escape and Anti-Vision," pp. 90-106. Cf. also Thomas Pynchon, *V*(New York: J. B. Lippincott, 1963).

[69]Robert Sklar, "The New Novel, U.S.A.: Thomas Pynchon," *Nation,* Vol. 205, No. 9(September 25, 1967), p. 70.

[70]C. G. Gros, "Review of *V*," *Best Sellers* (April 1, 1936), p. 23.

[71]R. H. W. Dillard, *"V"* in *Masterplots, 1963* (Carbondale, Ill.: Southern Illinois, University Press, 1966), p. 286.

[72]Hunt, "Comic Escape and Anti-Vision," p. 107.

which takes for granted that the world is without discoverable purposes or goals. This type of literature, therefore, devotes itself to random procedures and gives up pattern and form so it may be truly open to the turbulent incoherence of reality.[73]

Transitional men between the Classical-Moderns and Post-Modern radicals include Saul Bellow, John Updike, William Styron, Philip Roth, and Bernard Malamud.

As theologians, lay and professional, we are frustrated as we confront this literature which does not focus on the ultimate issues as did the Classical-Moderns.[74] A strange new *silence* has settled on the field of literature. Is this a cleansing of the old half-truths to make ready for a new intense hunger and receptivity? Is this zero point in literature a preparation for a radical new submission to the Creator who has provided for us a model of meaning and power and hope in Jesus Christ?

---

[73]Scott, *Negative Capability,* p. 48.

[74]Amos Wilder finds the Post-Modern novel lacking in the holism or total humanism of the biblical narratives. He makes this as a literary observation—not as a complaint that the novels do not present the biblical world-view or theology. Cf. Wilder, *The New Voice,* p. 75.

III

THEOLOGY AND CONTEMPORARY

DRAMA

Classical-Modern Drama

SHORTLY BEFORE WORLD WAR I there began a number of artistic movements that, taken together, initiated what is now popularly known as "modern" art. These movements include not only drama but such developments as Cubist painting, Stravinsky's *Rite of Spring,* Joyce's *Ulysses,* and Eliot's *The Waste Land.* This period of "Classical-Modern," as it is now oftentimes called, lasted through World War II and its aftermath. Since the late 1950's, we have witnessed a groping after a new direction—the "Post-Moderns."[1] Following the pattern utilized in evaluating literature, we will distinguish between Classical-Modern drama and Post-Modern drama.[2] Classical-Moderns chosen as representative include Eugene

---

[1]Tom F. Driver, *Romantic Quest and Modern Theory* (New York: Delacorte Press, 1970), p. 283.

[2]Note that Negative drama is the only type under consideration in this study. For consideration of Indirect drama (T. S. Eliot, Graham Greene, etc.) and Religious drama (Christopher Fry, Philip Turner, Charles Williams, Rutenborn, etc.) see Newport, "Questions Ministers Ask About Literature and Drama," pp. 31-47.

O'Neill, Arthur Miller, Tennessee Williams, and Jean Paul
Sartre.

EUGENE O'NEILL

The position of Eugene O'Neill as the leading American
dramatist has never been seriously questioned. In fact, American drama came to be taken seriously in Europe only with
Eugene O'Neill (1888-1953). From 1920 to the present,
O'Neill has towered over all other American playwrights by
virtue of his forcefulness, his variety, his thematic grandeur,
and his near-tragic view of man. No other American playwright has received as much attention both here and abroad
or as large an audience over the span of two generations as has
O'Neill. He won the Nobel Prize for literature in 1936. Four
of his plays won Pulitzer Prizes—*Beyond the Horizon* (1920);
Anna Christie (1922); *Strange Interlude* (1928); and *Long
Day's Journey into Night* (1957). Other plays became well-
known: *Desire Under the Elms, Mourning Becomes Electra,
The Hairy Ape,* and *The Iceman Cometh.* Apart from O'Neill,
the American theater in the '40s and '50s was dominated by
the reputations of Arthur Miller and Tennessee Williams, with
William Inge somewhere in the running.[3]

A representative work of O'Neill is one of his later plays,
The Iceman Cometh (1939). This is a powerful naturalistic
drama which gives us a slice of life on skid row. At the heart
of the play is O'Neill's statement about the absoluteness of
death. For him, death has priority over life.[4]

The arrangement of *The Iceman Cometh* reveals O'Neill's
power as a dramatist. The barroom group awaits the arrival
of their hero—Hickey—the iceman. On this visit he tells
them that they can realize their pipe dreams if they will act.
The barroom group goes out but they come back with dreams

---

[3]Driver, *Romantic Quest and Modern Theory,* pp. 285, 292, 307, 308.
Authoritative biographical works on O'Neill include: Arthur and Barbara
Gelb, *O'Neill* (New York: Harper and Row, 1960-62) and Louis Sheaffer,
O'Neill: Son and Playwright (Boston: Little, Brown and Co., 1968).
[4]There is some indication that O'Neill's concern changed in the later
thirties and forties from a struggle with God to a struggle with himself.
Cf. Robert Brustein, *The Theatre of Revolt: An Approach to Modern
Drama* (Boston: Little, Brown, and Company, 1962), p. 331.

shattered by "what's out there," which is what he intended. Hickey did not anticipate, however, the frightful relapse which followed the action of the barroom crowd and their return. Parritt, the radical, realizes that only death will relieve him of his guilt, and so he commits suicide. Larry, the philosophical character, becomes a real convert to death. Hickey finally confesses the murder of his own wife and gives himself up to death.

As a Freudian, O'Neill has Hickey wanting the absolute freedom of the "Id," to let himself go. But he can't, because the "Super-Ego" stands in the way. Hickey decides that he can get peace if he gets rid of his "Super-Ego." But this is suicide. Here is the battle of death and life, and death wins. The only absolute O'Neill can find is death.[5]

In *The Iceman Cometh* and other plays, O'Neill sees man in a tragic position. If a person follows the line of convention, he will remain unproductive and unloved. If he follows his creative instincts, he will be misunderstood and tortured. *The Iceman Cometh* portrays man as yearning for a world of imaginary values and yet finding himself incapable of casting off the weights pulling him toward death.[6]

In Act 2 of O'Neill's play, *Long Day's Journey into Night,* Edmund (O'Neill's alter ego) is in an argument with his father. Edmund shouts out, "Then Nietzsche must be right. God is Dead: of his pity for man hath God died."[7] For O'Neill, the old God had died and the new "gods" of science and materialism did not satisfy. Man, therefore, was left without any solution to satisfy his desire for meaning in life and to give him hope in his fear of death.

O'Neill's funeral was symbolically an interment into nothingness. There was the "silent void" as the task was undertaken with no clergy or religious ceremony. Only his wife, Carlotta, his secretary, and his doctor attended. There were

---

[5]Tom F. Driver, "On the Late Plays of Eugene O'Neill," in *Man in the Modern Theatre,* ed. Nathan A. Scott, Jr. (Richmond, Va.: John Knox Press, 1965), pp. 40-57.

[6]Heinrich Straumann, *American Literature in the Twentieth Century* (New York: Harper and Row, 1965), pp. 185-187.

[7]Eugene O'Neill, *Long Day's Journey into Night* (New Haven: Yale University Press, 1956), p. 78.

no prayers, hymns, or spoken words. All this was requested by O'Neill.[8] The funeral seemed to be in keeping with the tragedy of his earlier years. He was born in a hotel room in New York to a mother who was a victim of morphine drugs. His brother, Jamie, became an alcoholic. His oldest son, Eugene, Jr., committed suicide in 1950. His other son, Shane, became an alcoholic. What a contrast to the Christian faith, which through the revelation in Jesus Christ has learned that God can be trusted to bring meaning and victory in this life and bring about the proper fulfillment beyond death! Despair, nihilism, and death are robbed of their power to destroy creativity, freedom, and hope.

O'Neill can be called a Classical-Modern, however, because all of his heroes, despite their failure, guilt, and alienation, desperately try to find some sort of sense or order or peace in their lives, if only for brief moments.

ARTHUR MILLER

Arthur Miller is a compelling dramatist with a profound concern for the human condition. The social realism of his plays is strong, as can be seen in *All My Sons,* which has economic implications, and *The Crucible,* which has political overtones.

In 1953 Miller won the Pulitzer Prize for *Death of a Salesman.* This powerful play uses a synthesis of many varied forms of the theater including Realism, Expressionism, and Naturalism. *Death of a Salesman* embraces both determinism and the overwhelming power of a common man's will. It contends for individual responsibility.[9] The fault eventually lies with Willy Loman himself in *Death of a Salesman* and in Eddie's character fault in *A View from the Bridge. After the Fall* has strongly autobiographical features and symbolizes man's love, despair, and self-examination in the modern world.[10]

---

[8]Gelb and Gelb, *O'Neill.* pp. 942f.
[9]Arthur Miller, *Arthur Miller's Collected Plays* (New York: The Viking Press, 1960), pp. 52-55.
[10]Donald Whittle, *Christianity and the Arts* (Philadelphia: Fortress Press, 1966), p. 116.

Miller also can be called a Classical-Modern. His plots are tightly drawn and his characters are clearly defined. His progression is linear—from a precise beginning through a distinguishable middle to an unambiguous end. Realism is dominant.

Arthur Miller's plays, according to Driver, have all of the mood and tone of profundity—in fact, *Death of a Salesman* is one of the most impressive mood pieces ever seen on the American stage. It, however, lacks real profundity. For Driver, American drama in the twentieth century, as a whole, has been impoverished by the lack of ontological depth and romantic irony. The patterns of narrative and of stage action which American drama arranges seldom seem to symbolize adequately a grappling with profound and ultimate problems. The distinction between what is illusory and what is real is not at home on the American stage. O'Neill and the early Tennessee Williams aside, the best American theater has come where deep substance is not asked for or appears only indirectly—that is, in comedy, in certain works of social protest, and in the musical. There is no important American tragicomedy. Edward Albee's work would be the nearest thing to it. Perhaps a longer shadow of suffering is a necessary prerequisite.[11]

TENNESSEE WILLIAMS

Tom Driver suggests that in Tennessee Williams' *A Streetcar Named Desire* a high point of international as well as of American postwar theater was reached. This 1947 play combined many of the finest elements of modern theater. These include the Chekhovian focus upon the quality of experience, the Strindbergian occupation with sexual violence and with expressionistic methods, the poetic revival in drama, the anti-illusionism of the Continental theater, and Pirandello's interest in illusion and reality. Moreover, Williams' locales and his characters were completely American. He made of them vehicles of expression for his fears about the decadence of society and society's violent animosity toward things tender,

---

[11]Driver, *Romantic Quest and Modern Theory*, pp. 311f., 321f.

sensitive, and human. Unfortunately, he later over-emphasized violence and became too shrill.[12]

The background of Tennessee Williams, who undoubtedly will go down in history as one of the two most powerful American playwrights of the twentieth century, is important for understanding his art.[13] He was born in 1914 in his grandfather's Episcopal rectory in Mississippi. His father was a cavalier traveling salesman who was gone much of the time. Upon moving to the tenement section of St. Louis, Williams lived what he called a trapped existence. After attending several colleges, he became the vagabond poet of the theater.[14] An interesting development is seen in the fact that he was baptized into the Roman Catholic church in January of 1969.

Williams own experiences helped to give him a sense of compassion for frustrated persons trapped in a highly competitive, commercial world. His iconoclasm and Bohemian interests were evidently a reaction to his mother's influence and to conservative Southern life.[15]

Tennessee Williams writes of the familiar existentialistic problems: alienation, failure in human communication, the loneliness of life. In most of his dramas, tenderness and compassion are seen as a source of healing. He searches for grace in a universe touched by evil on every side. But, as a whole, he does not find saving mercy in the heart of man or God.[16]

Summer and Smoke and *Cat on a Hot Tin Roof* confront the struggle of the spirit and the flesh which awaits those who decide to live in the present. John in *Summer and Smoke* finally shows that the choice of the spiritual does not necessitate a forsaking of the physical or of reality. This play considers the spiritual dimensions of life in an incarnational rather than a gnostic manner. *Cat on a Hot Tin Roof* is a protest

[12]Ibid., pp. 309f.

[13]Sy Kahn, "Through a Glass Menagerie Darkly: The World of Tennessee Williams," *Modern American Drama: Essays in Criticism*, ed. by William E. Taylor (DeLand, Fla.: Everett/Edwards, Inc., 1968), p. 71.

[14]Nancy M. Tischler, *Tennessee Williams: Rebellious Puritan* (New York: McGraw-Hill Book Company, Inc., 1961), pp. 16f.

[15]Ibid., pp. 38-39, 60. Cf. also Signi Lenea Falk, *Tennesee Williams* (New York: Twayne Publishers, Inc., 1961), pp. 163-165.

[16]Padovano, *American Culture and the Quest for Christ*, pp. 198f.

against death and sterility. It builds its hope for life on life.[17]

Suddenly Last Summer is a disturbing portrayal of a universe penetrated with evil and doomed to death. Sebastian Venable suffers a cannibalistic death because he lives in a carnivorous universe presided over by a savage God. In *Sweet Bird of Youth* innocence is more subtly corrupted and there remains a possibility of rebirth through the love of others.[18]

Tennessee Williams is intensely concerned with the conflict between imagination (illusion) and reality as seen in *The Glass Menagerie* and *A Streetcar Named Desire*. His dramatic work has popularly been called "poetic realism." Many of his chief characters, who cannot distinguish between illusion and reality, tend to break down. Notable are Laura in *The Glass Menagerie* and Blanche in *A Streetcar Named Desire*. He emphasizes the falseness of relations and lack of communication.[19]

Despite his compassion and tenderness, in plays such as *Baby Doll* and *Cat on a Hot Tin Roof,* Williams' characters seem to be hopeless and determined. He reflects a cultural behaviorism and determinism which flows out of a pessimistic stream of social Darwinism.

Has Williams moved beyond his earlier naturalism in more recent years? Some contend that he has. The numinous breaks through more often. In a more recent play, *The Night of the Iguana,* a sense of community, of men's need of love and each other comes through in a powerful way.[20]

He has written few plays since his conversion to the Catholic faith. One is entitled, *In the Bar of a Tokyo Hotel.* An article in *Esquire* suggests that the symbolism of "in the bar" might mean "on the Cross" and that the "Tokyo Hotel" is "the gates of heaven."[21]

In any case, Williams is a master of dialectical drama. He has a special appeal for the rootless urbanites who struggle with both an explicit and implicit determinism. He can be

[17]Ibid., pp. 207f., 208, 210, 218.
[18]Ibid., pp. 212, 200.
[19]Straumann, *American Literature in the Twentieth Century*, p. 203.
[20]John R. Killinger, Jr., "The Climate of Doubt and Faith in Contemporary Literature," *Baptist Faculty Paper*, 10, no. 2 (Spring, 1967), pp. 2, 5.
[21]Donald Newlove, "A Dream of Tennessee Williams," *Esquire* magazine, LXXII (November, 1969), p. 178.

called a Classical-Modern for he does struggle to bring some hope and order to man's chaotic world.

JEAN PAUL SARTRE

Jean Paul Sartre of France is a transition dramatist (and novelist and philosopher) between the Classical-Moderns and the Post-Moderns. On the surface, there appear to be few influences in his early life to help create the rebellion that would later be portrayed in his writings. He was born in 1905 into a liberal Catholic family and was a good student. It is known, however, that his grandfather had a crushing academic zeal and forced young Jean Paul into early adulthood. He lived with books from the age of seven and felt *excluded* from the world of other boys. In 1938, Sartre published a novel called *Nausea* which expressed some of his basic ideas. Perhaps his experience as a German prisoner in 1940-41 helped to crystallize radical tendencies.[22]

Sartre affirms that there is no rationality and that the universe is absurd. The only reality is that which proceeds from the self in its free encounter with the world and with other selves. What is beyond the self has no meaning in itself. Thus the universe is "absurd." Sartre did not originate this idea but borrowed it from Nietzsche and the early Heidegger. He did, however, enunciate the idea and dramatically forced it into the human consciousness.[23]

Nausea, as experienced by Rocquentin, the main character in the novel *Nausea,* is an experience which characterizes consciousness when it becomes aware of itself as nothingness. Nausea was caused by efforts to read meaning where there is none.[24] Nausea is related to the viscous—the moist, formless, and sticky. Fertility (including females) is revolting because it perpetuates existence for which there is no reason.

---

[22]Fredrich Lumley, *Trends in Twentieth Century Drama* (London: Barrie and Rockliff, 1956), pp. 154-156. Cf. also Jean-Paul Sartre, *The Words,* tr. by Bernard Frechtman (New York: G. Braziller, 1946), pp. 49, 19, 153, 135.

[23]Driver, *Romantic Quest and Modern Theory,* p. 374.

[24]Frederick Patka, *Existential Thinkers and Thought* (New York: Philosophical Library, 1962), pp. 132f.

A person, however, according to Sartre, can and must authenticate himself in an absurd world by an act of the will. The situation and the context are relatively unimportant— act! Without God in the world, man is thrown back upon himself, both for maintenance and creation. Man is condemned to be free. Existence precedes essence. For Sartre, the devotion of a religious man to God is a retreat from the responsibility of forging the self by the self. It is not difficult to understand why the Japanese intellectual, conditioned by Buddhism, has found Sartre's thought so attractive.

Drama is used by Sartre to present his philosophy and defend it. *No Exit* is a play in which the characters come to understand that life, death, and hell are all absurd. The most absurd reality of all is that "hell is other people." Hell is not a consequence in time but is an enduring presence. There is no help, no hope—not even in other persons who must spend eternity together in a room of hell. In *The Flies,* the absurdity of life is seen vividly in the symbol of the flies. All life is seen as decay. Slimy existence is seen as the basic form of life. On this decaying soil, vermin swarm and larvae fatten and develop into flies.

Unfortunately, Sartre lacks the humor of some of the Post-Moderns and the pathos and compassion of men like Tennessee Williams. Scott calls Sartre an antitype of the comic imagination. He recoils into disgust, as is seen in *Nausea.* As already noted, the hero Rocquentin reaches a mental state in which everything seems disheveled, messy, and obscene. Through his character, Sartre reveals his profound distrust of creation. The comedian always calls such a distrust into question. The comic man bears the burden of human finitude in a finite world with no such sense of desperate entrapment. He can affirm the world. The Christian imagination, therefore, has more sympathy for the affirmative quality in the comic vision than it does for the negativity of Sartre.[25]

Sartre creates his play *The Flies* from the familiar Greek myth of Orestes in the tradition of Aeschylus, Sophocles, and Euripides. He seeks, however, to transform the ancient myth

---

[25]Scott, *Broken Center,* pp. 26f., 104, 108.

of Orestes from a tragedy of fatality into a tragedy of free-dom. Although he is an atheist, Sartre does offer a way out—affirm freedom—even if it means joining a contemporary parallel to the French Resistance. In *The Devil and the Good Lord,* in one of the most sacrilegious dialogues in drama, Goetz turns to himself, saying, "I am alone and I must decide for myself."[26]

Ironically, Sartre himself did not use avant-garde theatrical forms when he composed his plays. He wrote plays, only mildly experimental in form, which emphasized ideas. His first play, *The Flies* (1940), is his most radical in form. *No Exit* (1944) is a drawing room play even though he uses symbolic realism. He is closer to Ibsen than Chekhov and uses bourgeois theater to attack bourgeois conceptions. Sartre belongs to the spirit of the World War II period and is a bridge in ideas (if not in theater) to the Post-Modern play-wrights.[27] Thus, although he has Post-Modern tendencies, Sartre must be classified as a Classical-Modern.

Post-Modern Drama

Drama also has its Post-Modern developments. These new directions, such as those which are exemplified in the "Theater of the Absurd," have anticipations or forerunners in earlier drama. In Buechner, Strindberg, Chekhov, and Piran-dello there was an emphasis on imbalance and unresolved tension.

BACKGROUND DRAMATISTS

Buechner (1813-1837) was haunted by a sense of cosmic alienation. He is the first of the modern dramatists to engage in a stripping away of post-Renaissance idealization. In *Danton's Death,* Buechner expresses this twilight of faith in one scene: "The world is chaos. Nothingness is the world god yet to be born." Although chronologically *Danton's Death* is in the modern period of drama, in spirit and technique it be-

---

[26]Allen Lewis, *The Contemporary Theater* (New York: Crown Publishing Co., 1962), pp. 205-210.
[27]Driver, *Romantic Quest and Modern Theory,* pp. 376-378.

longs to the Post-Modern phase.[28] In *Danton's Death,* first performed in 1902, Buechner shattered classical structures of drama and developed episodic drama in order to express the modern spirit. It is significant that *Danton's Death* was chosen as the opening play for the new Lincoln Theater Center in New York City.

Tom Driver contends that Chekhov (1860-1904) gave a completely new balance and emphasis to the three sequential modes—purposeful action, consequent endurance of suffering, and eventual gain of new perception—of the Aristotelian pattern of drama. The mode of passion or of experience undergone is paramount or central. He further combines the tragic and the comic into tragicomedy. For example, the climax in *Uncle Vanya* misfires—it is absurd and comically abortive. Chekhov prepared the way for Pirandello and Brecht and Beckett and Ionesco.[29]

Pirandello (1867-1936) stood between realism, for which theater is an imitation of life, and that late development for which theater is an imitation of consciousness.[30] In Pirandello's *Henry IV* the concern is away from objective incidents towards inward experience.

Driver suggests that Bertolt Brecht (1898-1956) shares with Pirandello and other modern dramatists a profound sense of human self-alienation. But he differs in rejecting religious, existential, or psychological causes. As a Communist, he ascribes it to contradictions in the structure of society and to man's failure to think his way out of these.[31]

In the plays of these Post-Modern forerunners such as Buechner, Chekhov, and Pirandello are seen loosely knit plots with little or no climax. These plays proceed in rather haphazard, often circular movements. The crucial thing is the development of a new mood or climate in drama.[32]

[28]Ibid., pp. 31-35.
[29]Ibid., pp. 223, 227, 247. Cf. also Eric Bentley, *In Search of Theater* (New York: Vintage, 1954), pp. 322-343.
[30]Ibid., p. 393. Cf. also Domenico Vittorini, *The Drama of Luigi Pirandello* (New York: Dover, 1957).
[31]Ibid., p. 435. Cf. also John Willett, *The Theatre of Bertolt Brecht* (New York: New Directions, 1959).
[32]Nelvin Vos, *The Drama of Comedy: Victim and Victor* (Richmond, Va.: John Knox Press, 1966), p. 54.

THEATER OF THE ABSURD

The contemporary expression of the Post-Modern spirit has been designated as the "Theater of the Absurd." (Absurd in this connection does not mean silly or ridiculous but devoid of purpose in a metaphysical sense.) Since the appearance of Martin Esslin's book, *The Theater of the Absurd,* in 1961, the term "absurdists" has been applied to the "Paris School" or "the new playwrights." In addition to the four to be discussed in this study—Beckett, Ionesco, Pinter, and Albee—Esslin includes sixteen others, the most notable of whom are Adamov, Genet, Günter Grass, Kopit, and Jack Gelber. In historical perspective, the important point is that all twenty dramatists broke with the bourgeois forms of the theater and constructed plays distinguished by their own concrete images of the stage.[33]

Drama was not seen as the imitation of action or of life, but as the imitation of theater and of consciousness. As painting freed itself from photography and history and turned to pure form and color, in this movement the theater has turned to its own techniques, divorced from rational meaning. Ionesco conceived the idea that he would restore to the theater its visual and primitive qualities. He would exalt stages, properties, and the moving architecture of scenic images.[34]

JEAN GENET AND ANTONIN ARTAUD

For Tom Driver, it is in Jean Genet that the modern theater has realized most fully what it means to emphasize the imitation of consciousness. He was fascinated with words and the purity of ritual form. He was concerned with essences, fatalities, and magical transformations. Notable works include *Deathwatch, The Maids, The Balcony, The Blacks,* and *The Screens.* These works record the pilgrimage of a criminal-saint who went out from his prison. At first he was only

---

[33]Martin Esslin, *The Theatre of the Absurd* (Garden City, N.Y.: Anchor Books, Doubleday, 1961), p. xxi.

[34]Eugene Ionesco, "Discovering the Theatre," tr. by L. C. Pronko, in Robert W. Corrigan, ed., *Theatre in the Twentieth Century* (New York: Grove, 1963), pp. 91, 85, 88.

interested in images and rituals. In later days, he was more concerned with reality.[35]

As has already been pointed out, modern developments in literature and drama have one common element: philosophical skepticism about the adequacy of the human mind to know and embrace reality. Of course, the scientific method has been successful in dealing with the natural world. In turn, the subjective humanities have been intimidated. Thus there is a split in the human consciousness. The theater uses irony to speak of this split consciousness and alienation. It has adopted expressionistic and surrealistic techniques to express depth. Jean Cocteau (1889-1963) is a well-known French surrealist who is an example of one who used this approach. (Cf. *The Eiffel Tower Wedding Party, Orpheus, The Infernal Machine.*)[36]

An important figure in Post-Modern drama is Antonin Artaud (1896-1948). He was a visionary ahead of his time who saw the theater as a mirror of the human consciousness imprisoned within itself. Furthermore, the theater arises from itself and goes toward itself. It has no essential relation to life outside.

Philosophically, the negative protest against the theater and religion of the past was embodied in existentialists like Jean Paul Sartre. But the real iconoclasts are known as the "absurdist" playwrights. It took the threat of atomic annihilation to bring the protest to the point where it could change the very notion of theatrical form.[37]

Artaud, for example, insisted in his various manifestos that Western theater had been off the track for centuries and should now endeavor to become a caldron of magic, violence, and extreme action. The audience should not be allowed to sit as mere spectators. They should be aroused, seduced, attacked, or assaulted into response and participation. Artaud affirmed that the theater should deal in the raw, abrasive aspects of existence.[38] He has been called the originator of

---

[35]Driver, *Romantic Quest and Modern Theory,* pp. 437ff., 452, 454.
[36]Ibid., pp. 347f., 350-353.
[37]Ibid., pp. 361, 368, 374.
[38]Antonin Artaud, *The Theatre and Its Double,* trans. by Mary Caroline Richards (New York: Grove Press, 1958), p. 74.

the "theater of cruelty." His influence can be seen in the Beck-Molina "Living Theater," in which the actors often harass and insult the patrons. Peter Weiss in *Marat/Sade* and Jean Genet in *The Blacks* reflect his influence, as do some movies and television shows. He also inspired Ionesco and Pinter.[39] Artaud did not want just to *examine* how hatred, pain, ambition, jealousy, and fear operate in the lives of particular characters. He wanted the theater to *propel* the spectators into a direct encounter with these forces.[40]

For Artaud, theater should also propel man into fantasy and dreaming. The past must be destroyed in order to create the future.[41] Creativity, not the communication of ideas, was to be the main emphasis. Words and movements were to be selected—not first for their idea content—but for their sound and emotional resonance. Man was to be stirred into life and creation. The past is not to be continued or reduplicated. Artaud wants men to feel, shape, encounter, and recreate. He is so compelled to seek the new that he has disgust for what is. In some ways, Artaud illustrates the anti-ideological and visionary quality of some of the student radicals of today.[42]

As already indicated, Artaud has had considerable influence on the "Living Theater" which begat such productions as *Hair* and *Salvation*. Neutrality towards such theater seems impossible. Some say it has conviction and energy and ignites key issues such as youth versus age, love, the draft, race, drugs, and war. Others call it "Modcom"—the commercial exploitation of modernity without regard for traditional dramatic art.

CHARACTERISTICS OF THE THEATER OF THE ABSURD

From a more philosophical perspective, the men of the "Theater of the Absurd" carry on to its logical implications

---

[39]Cox, *Feast of Fools,* p. 35. Cf. also Robert Brustein, *The Theatre of Revolt: An Approach to Modern Drama* (Boston: Little, Brown and Company, 1962-64).

[40]Artaud, *The Theatre and Its Double,* p. 74. Cf. also Jack Hirschman, ed., *Antonin Artaud Anthology,* 2nd ed., rev. (San Francisco: City Lights, 1965) and Bettina L. Knapp, *Antonin Artaud: Man of Vision* (New York: David Lewis, 1969).

[41]Ibid., p. 78.

[42]Cox, *Feast of Fools,* pp. 36f., 39, 41.

the theses of Sartre—the non-existence of God or a rational order behind the world of "appearances" and the non-existence of a rational ego or substantial self. They actually disclose the absurd. These men, to use a metaphor of the theater, pull off the masks. As Ionesco has said, ". . . cut off from his religious, metaphysical and transcendent roots, man is lost: all his actions become senseless, absurd, useless."[43]

The disorderliness of the universe, according to the "Absurd" dramatists, is no longer something with which human beings cope, but something they merely accept and experience. Man is no longer seen as a center of intelligence with a mandate for making sense of the impressions he receives from the world around him. Man is not the great unifier we once thought he was. He exerts no force on occurrences of life to bring them into a meaningful relationship. Man experiences things mechanically and serially.[44]

As in the case of Post-Modern literature, in this avant-garde drama the traditional properties of character and story are minimized. The world is presented as "just there" and not amenable to ordering principles. The stagecraft is more abstract. It is like the mechanical interactions of human puppets. Very few generalizations are advanced. What the characters do is not done out of rational considerations of motive and intent. Words are devalued and the syntax is abnormal. The presentation is a radically situational tableau of happenings.[45] Anything can happen next. There is no gradual revelation or gradual completion of a unifying pattern. The avant-garde theater becomes a mirror of the alienated and meaningless state of modern man. The language used is commonplace but oftentimes it is planned that communication will not occur.[46]

In the Theater of the Absurd all human relationships are

[43]Eugene Ionesco, "Dans Les Armes de la Ville," *Cahiers de la Compagnie Madeleine Fenaud-Jean-Louis Barrault,* (Paris, no. 20, October, 1957); quoted in Martin Esslin, *The Theater of the Absurd* (Garden City, N.J.: Doubleday Anchor Books), p. xix.

[44]John Killinger, "Death and Transcendence in Contemporary Literature," *Perspectives on Death* (Nashville: Abingdon Press, 1969), p. 157.

[45]Nathan A. Scott, Jr., *Negative Capability* (New Haven: Yale University Press, 1969), p. 45.

[46]Richard E. Sherrell, *The Human Image: Avant-Garde and Christian* (Richmond, Va.: John Knox Press, 1969), pp. 33f.

questioned including those between man and woman. Marriage is more often a destructive state. Since it is a theater of skepticism about all things human, it requires that nothing more fancy or complicated be presented than "little" facts. The human entropy in this drama is analogous to the entropy which some claim is occurring in the physical world—the orderly is becoming more random and disorderly—toward extinction.[47]

The biblical idea is that humans made in the image of God are to exercise creative dominion over the other orders of life and existence under God's sovereignty. To some extent this emphasis is implied or reflected in the Classical-Moderns. In the Theater of the Absurd this is upended. Man is at the mercy of virtually everything in the world. Beckett's characters are sometimes clowns and buffoons who cannot keep their hats on. Ionesco's characters are often crowded off the stage by objects such as eggs, mushrooms, furniture, and growing corpses. They easily merge with the animal world and become chickens or rhinoceroses.[48]

Transcendence has been dissipated in the Post-Modern dramatists. A sense of mystery about life or death is virtually absent. Life is as colorless as Sheol. Many see these dramatists as heralding a kind of zero age. Even suicide would be meaningless because man has become a mere scholarly vegetable.[49]

SAMUEL BECKETT

Samuel Beckett is the best-known playwright of the Theater of the Absurd. *Waiting For Godot, Endgame,* and *Krapp's Last Tape* have puzzled and entranced audiences—especially in college and university circles.

Waiting for Godot (1953) is not only a masterpiece, but also the quintessence of modern tragicomedy, an achievement that contributed, no doubt, to Beckett's being awarded, in 1969, the Nobel Prize for Literature. All of Beckett's plays

---

[47]Killinger, "Death and Transcendence in Contemporary Literature," p. 159.
[48]Ibid., p. 159.
[49]Ibid., p. 161.

are "games" for actors. In fact, one play is named *Play* (1963). When Beckett implies that life is a game, he means that it is made up of routines and that it is just something to do. Games become a substitute for loss of purpose. We are all clowns (or servants) wondering if our "bit" is sufficiently long to fill up the time allotted to us. Thus, the "routine" takes the place of the plot. A "shadow" plot exists which is usually seen in terms of waiting for what will *perhaps* never take place.[50]

Beckett makes the audience realize that modern man tends to interpret life as a plotless sequence of events. Theater becomes a ritual having no other meaning than its own form. But Beckett's form is superb, showing fine command of language. In a highly simplified way, Beckett is able in a play such as *Waiting for Godot* to represent on the stage the verbal, physical, and psychic notions that belong to our endurance of time. He verbalizes and portrays the consciousness of many Western men who are exhausted and bored and longing for death.[51]

Beckett is serious in his work, and his art is a match for his vision. He goes deeper than satire and irony to a tragic encounter with modern man struggling with his self-doubt and tormented by a logic that has no hold on things. In the discourse of his characters, there is frequently an obsession with number schemes, mathematical series, and computations which always end in zero or a surd. At the same time the craving for a human voice is a recurrent theme. He explores the gulf between the impersonal in human life and the human voice. And he pushes the dilemma to the utmost limit.[52]

Samuel Beckett's life reflects his plays and vice versa. Born in 1906 as an Irishman, he left Ireland in 1932 for France and has lived there since that time. For him Ireland was oppressive and anti-intellectual. He left the Anglican church finding it "irksome."[53] He told Peggy Guggenheim, who pur-

---

[50]Driver, *Romantic Quest and Modern Theory,* pp. 386-389.
[51]Ibid., p. 389.
[52]Wilder, *The New Voice,* pp. 148f., 162, 175.
[53]Haskell Black and Robert G. Shedd, eds., *Masters of Modern Drama* (New York: Random House, 1962), pp. 1102f.

sued him (as did Joyce's daughter), that he was dead and
had no feelings that were human.[54] A terribly private person,
Beckett fled Paris when he learned that he was being considered for a Nobel Prize. He was finally reached in Tunis and
said that he supposed that there was nothing he could do about
it if the Swedish Academy had decided to give him the prize.[55]
In his own personal life, as in his characters, life is seen as
existential nothingness and unfulfilled search for community.
His is a metaphysics of boredom. Time is a burden. Events
are meaningless.[56]

It was *Waiting For Godot* that catapulted Beckett and the
Absurd dramatists into public notice. In it the characters
merely sit, waiting for Godot—who never comes. The play
must be seen to be appreciated—conceptualization is inadequate. This play evokes a world in which despair and defeat
are so absolute as to be almost beyond the possibility of
dramatization. In this drama man is not at home in the world,
he is waiting hopelessly for significance to meet him. Man is a
being in relationship—he cannot be isolated—but he is. But
above all, *Waiting For Godot* transports a person into the
feeling of absurdity. The style is not realistic—but grotesque.[57]

The whole setting of *Waiting For Godot* breeds despair.
There is vacillation between much despair and a tiny spark of
hope. The use of biblical references wherein hope had for-
merely been placed is a foil against which to play up the despair
and absurdity of today. Beckett uses Saturday after Good Fri-
day as the time of the play to indicate despair—to ask whether
the Sunday of Easter is worth waiting for. Over against the
biblical ideas of purpose and community are placed non-
purpose and estrangement. In *Engame* Hamm tells Clov to

[54]Martin Esslin, "Samuel Beckett: The Search for Self," in *Samuel Beckett: A Collection of Critical Essays*, ed., Martin Esslin (Englewood Cliffs, N.J.: Prentice-Hall, Inc., 1965), p. 16.
[55]"Views from the Wasteland," *Newsweek Magazine*, November 3, 1969, p. 54.
[56]Dan O. Via, Jr., *Samuel Beckett's Waiting For Godot* (New York: The Seabury Press, 1968), p. 19.
[57]Sherrell, *The Human Image*, pp. 45, 62. Cf. also Nathan A. Scott, Jr., *Craters of the Spirit* (Washington, D.C.: Corpus Books, 1968), p. 176 and William R. Mueller, "Samuel Beckett's Long Saturday: To Wait or Not to Wait?" in *Man in the Modern Theatre*, Nathan A. Scott, Jr., ed., p. 78.

quickly kill the flea on him (or perhaps it is a crab) because the flea might be the base for starting pitiful humanity all over again. The greatest laughter comes when men's highest hopes are disappointed. For Beckett's characters there is little but misery and lack of freedom. Man is lonely, separate, and has no communication.[58]

But there is some mysterious impulse which impels the characters to wait, even though the odds, according to Beckett, seem heavily against success. If "salvation" is to come, Godot must renounce his inactivity and reveal himself.[59] Some interpreters of *Waiting For Godot,* such as Kay Baxter, believe that behind the drama there is a hidden meaning. Godot (seen as a reference to God) is hidden, yet is revealed in the actual events of the sacrificial character, Lucky. For Baxter, this is a disguised passion play of God's supreme event of history, which gives meaning to all existence.[60] The majority of Christian critics, however, see *Waiting For Godot* as a picture of the world 500 years before Christ. For Christians, the waiting period is over. But not for Beckett.

The many other plays of Beckett are also filled with characters who are half blind, stinking, crippled, or crawling. They live in garbage cans or insane asylums. They are impotent and incoherent. They are lonely and without connection. *Endgame* portrays a world where the traditional props of Western civilization—family cohesion, parental and marital love, faith in God, and artistic appreciation and creation—are gone.[61] In the mime which follows *Endgame,* the single actor frantically chases whistles and is thrown back after each chase. Then, with whistles still blowing, various objects are lowered. But they are snatched upward each time he reaches for them. At last he simply remains lying on his side—staring. When objects are lowered before his face, he now disregards them and stares at his hands. It is the world of zero.[62]

[58] Mueller, "Samuel Beckett's Long Saturday," pp. 80-96.
[59] Ibid., p. 97.
[60] Kathleen Mary Baxter, *Contemporary Theater and the Christian Faith* (New York: Abingdon Press, 1964), pp. 9-11.
[61] Black and Shedd, eds., *Masters of Modern Drama,* p. 1103.
[62] Scott, *Craters of the Spirit,* pp. 176, 195.

EUGENE IONESCO

Seldom in the history of drama has a playwright known the spectacular rise to world renown which came to Eugene Ionesco from 1956 to 1961. The revival of *The Chairs* suddenly attracted attention. Within five years he was acclaimed throughout the Western world. Born in Rumania in 1912, he has spent most of his life in France. Always controversial, it must be said that he is strikingly original both in subject and form.[63] Furthermore, he is one of the most available of the "Absurd" dramatists. He has written widely concerning his own work.

Historically speaking, Ionesco is affiliated with the subjective theater of German Expressionism, to which he adds black humor and the preoccupations of French Surrealism. Philosophically, he is close to the existentialists, looking at life as absurd, because unexplainable.

Ionesco completely rejects the European theater of the past. He advances in its place a dramatic style that discards external action as much as possible and flouts the realistic theater.[64] He uses a series of states of consciousness instead of specific plots. His theater is much like abstract painting dealing with form and color rather than with recognizable objects.[65]

In contrast to Sartre and Brecht, Ionesco is opposed to ideological plays. He is committed to non-commitment. The entire terrain of life and dreams, including wonder, fantasy, and violence, are explored. There is the utilization of exaggeration, caricature, farce, parody, the brutal, the outrageous, and the unendurable in order to detach men from their routine.[66]

A significant contribution of Ionesco lies in the fact that he has sought to give to his plays the very theatrical structure of his ideas. If the world is inhuman, then use robots. If the physi-

---

[63]Leonard C. Pronko, *Eugene Ionesco* (New York: Columbia University Press, 1965), p. 3. Cf. also Leonard C. Pronko, *Avant-Garde: The Experimental Theater in France* (Berkeley, Calif.: University of California Press, 1962).

[64]Hugh Dickinson, *Myth on the Modern Stage* (Urbana, Illinois: University of Illinois Press, 1969), p. 339.

[65]Pronko, *Eugene Ionesco,* pp. 7f.

[66]Ibid., pp. 5f.

cal denies the spiritual, then let the properties slowly dominate the characters. If language is worn out, then use clichés or slogans or pure agglomerates of sound.[67]

Variations from the serious to the ridiculous are the trademarks of Ionesco. The comic is the most powerful medium to convey his vision of the desperate and tragic absurdity of man's existence. In fact, the comic alone gives man the strength to bear the tragedy of existence.[68]

In his first plays, *The Bald Soprano* (1949) and *The Lesson* (1950), Ionesco pictures man as a comic victim of his own language and rationality. Originating with his own struggles to learn English from a primer, Ionesco explodes the small change and clichés of the average conversation.[69] *The Bald Soprano,* subtitled an "anti-play," utilized a simple plot, mechanical dehumanized characters, and exaggerated and absurd language. These were to become his characteristics— especially in his earlier plays. He used mechanical rhythms set up by the characters to suggest the underlying meaninglessness of most of our efforts to act and communicate. *The Lesson* shows us the danger of indoctrination. The professor becomes a monster and kills forty students with a metaphorical knife in one day.[70]

Logic is pursued by Ionesco relentlessly for a time, then exploded as if it were a breakable physical object. In *The Bald Soprano,* the proposition that if a doorbell rings it is because someone has rung, is examined at great length and finally abandoned as a useless conception. All relationships, whether of logic, grammar, custom, or marriage, are treated as a series of theatrical games whose rules may be changed at will.[71]

In *The Chairs, Jack,* and *The Future Is in Eggs,* Ionesco shows man as a victim of his social environment and of social institutions like marriage. *Jack,* or *The Submission* (1950) shows Jack, recalcitrant individualist, finally admitting that he

---

[67]Ibid., p. 13.
[68]Vos, *The Drama of Comedy,* p. 56. Cf. also Eugene Ionesco, "Notes and Counter Notes" in *Genet/Ionesco: The Theatre of the Double,* ed. Kelly Morris (New York: Bantam Books, Inc., 1969), pp. 117-141.
[69]Ibid., p. 56.
[70]Pronko, *Eugene Ionesco,* pp. 4, 13.
[71]Driver, *Romantic Quest and Modern Theory,* p. 381.

accepts the rules of society—that is, he likes fried potatoes with bacon. Jack and Roberta, in *The Future Is in Eggs* (1951), finally give in to their family's exhortation to raise children. In this play he uses the proliferation of physical matter encroaching on human presence—in this case, eggs. Surrealism, satire, and puns abound.[72] The theme of *The Chairs* is nothingness. There is a breakdown of language, and the bare stage becomes animated with pitiful dreams, repetitive memories, and inevitable mistakes. The subject of the play, as Ionesco described it in a letter to the director of the first performance, is not the moral disaster of two old people, but the chairs themselves. Once again matter is victorious over vital human presence. The play represents the absence of people, the absence of God, the unreality of the world, and metaphysical emptiness. The final scene presents a theatricalized sense of nothingness.[73]

In *The Chairs* Ionesco describes his vision of a world in which human action and self-sacrifice have no meaning. The old couple's destruction is meaningless. The long-awaited Messiah who arrives has no meaningful message and does not perform a significant redeeming action. Only the chairs remain. They materialize the solitude and overwhelm the human. The world of rationality is absurd. The physical world mocks all of man's attempts to control and master it.

In Ionesco's later plays, *The Killer* (1957) and *The Rhinoceros* (1959), man is represented as the comic victim of his finitude. A corpse dominates *Amédée* (1953), symbolizing the fact that the couple's dead, now meaningless, relationship is slowly destroying them, strangling them.[74] Its exaggerated size and presence provides a comic mood. *Rhinoceros* (1959) combines ultra-realism with fantasy and make-believe. Men are turned into rhinoceroses. Language, standards, and identity disappear. Socially, morally, ontologically man is not at home in the universe. Time and space are broken. Existence

---

[72]Pronko, *Eugene Ionesco*, pp. 14f.
[73]Vos, *The Drama of Comedy*, p. 56f. Cf. also Pronko, *Eugene Ionesco*, pp. 17f.
[74]Pronko, *Eugene Ionesco*, p. 21.

is chaotic.[75] *Rhinoceros* is an anti-Nazi play, but it is also an attack on collective hysteria and the epidemics which lurk beneath the surface of man's reason. Once again in this play Ionesco uses effectively proliferation in terms of the animal world.[76]

In *Victims of Duty* (1952), Ionesco has tried to drown the comic in the tragic. The emphasis is to be on a critical spirit that hovers between seriousness and lightness. The metaphysical assumptions of society such as logic and human relations are to be questioned. This desire to question all metaphysical affirmations is not just tragic or comic but a situation of tragicomedy. Ionesco leaves men suspended between two worlds. It is easy to note that his plays are scenes and events which are not according to pure reason or emotion but according to theatrical imagination. A person is led to the edge of consciousness and invited to peer into the darkness beyond. Then Ionesco pulls him back into the ambiguous but real world of everyday life. The play is filled with neither despair nor hope. It suggests eternal repetition. This theater pulls a person out of the realm of work and decision in order to force him to see life from a different perspective. It is an imitation of consciousness, not of life. Its strength is in its psychic rhythm—not in the validity of its ideas.[77]

Ionesco's world is even more hostile and menacing than Beckett's world of the absent God. Beckett's clowns worry and wait. Ionesco's couples are attacked, overwhelmed, and defeated. The frightening thing is that Ionesco often takes as his starting point man's actual tedious situations and then blows them up to grotesque proportions. These situations get out of control and monsters or vegetables take over. It is a parody of man's quest to find fulfillment.

The very texture of creation falls apart and becomes nonsensical. Ionesco believes man's problems are only beginning. He presents an image of man being crushed both by his internal world of reason and language and by his external world

[75]Vos, *The Drama of Comedy*, pp. 65f.
[76]Pronko, *Eugene Ionesco*, p. 33.
[77]Driver, *Romantic Quest and Modern Theory*, pp. 381-386.

of fellow humans and the materiál universe. In a poetic, laughable, and yet tragic way he has given us his vision.[78]

Here is the ultimate contrast to the classic view of a causal universe with rational language. The universe and life are absurd and language is meaningless. Since all is void of importance, says Ionesco, what is there to do but laugh at it?

HAROLD PINTER

Harold Pinter is a British representative of the "Absurd" dramatists. The son of a Jewish tailor, he was born in east London in 1930. Eight years a touring actor, he turned to playwrighting in 1957. His first commercial success was *The Caretaker* (1959). Several shorter plays were written for television, including *The Dwarfs, The Lover,* and *The Tea-Party.*[79]

The Homecoming (1965) has been highly acclaimed on Broadway and elsewhere. It is an unforgettable experience to sit through. The family theme is utilized in a cruelly inverted way. The characters are a father, his brother, his three sons, and his eldest son's wife. The pauses are almost unbearable. Beneath the restrained language is seething violence. His characters, especially Teddy, the American philosophy professor, are detached from all moral and human values. Is Teddy's wife, Ruth, an innocent woman being pressed into part-time prostitution, or is she already a bad character? The spectator never knows. For a person geared to explanations and cause and effect, it is horrifying. The playgoer is alienated. He wants to leave and yet he is fascinated. In one sense it is quite real—at least a person is not left with any fantasies.

The strange effect created by a play such as *The Homecoming* is caused by the fact that Pinter writes existential plays existentially. According to existentialism, a person does not come to the planet with an identity or an essence, he creates a

---

[78]Sherrell, *The Human Image,* p. 88.
[79]Walter Kerr, *Harold Pinter* (New York: Columbia University Press, 1967), pp. 46f. Cf. also Arnold Hinchliffe, *Harold Pinter* (New York: Twayne Publishing Co., Inc., 1967).

nature by adventure and free decisions. Walter Kerr affirms that Pinter is one of the few playwrights to present his plays in an actual existential sequence. He gives existence free rein. Concrete objects are handled as important. The plays create anxiety in the spectators. There seem to be few points of reference and no pattern. Cause and effect are neglected.[80]

In *The Homecoming,* Teddy, the professor husband, has everything fixed and organized. Ruth, the wife, however, does not accept her role as terminal. She moves on to be a "whore." Pinter uses the "whore" image because it is a symbol of continuing experience. The "whore" is what each new man makes of her.[81]

The uniqueness of Pinter as a playwright has been his success in constructing a series of present tense realities that are not dependent upon the usual conceptual frameworks. His plays are events, not just logical demonstrations. Oftentimes, however, he slips back into platonic categories. His male figures, for example, seem to be incapable of open and free action—they are predefined.[82]

From the Christian perspective, Pinter has only grasped a half-truth. Man does have freedom, but it is to be found in the context of the limits set by a personal Creator and within a created order. Man is to exercise his freedom and find fulfillment as a creature—not as creator. Although man is fallen, the loving Creator seeks to restore man to full freedom. Each person is unique and has a continuing identity—for good or bad—depending on responses to redemptive overtures.

EDWARD ALBEE

An American representative of the "Absurd" theater is Edward Albee. Born in 1928, Albee's life story has elements of absurdity. Adopted into a wealthy home, he was surrounded by every advantage. After expulsion from various fashionable

---

[80]Ibid., pp. 3, 5f., 9f., 19, 21. Cf. also William Barrett, *Irrational Man* (Garden City, N.Y.: Doubleday and Co., Inc., 1958), pp. 42-68.
[81]Ibid., pp. 34-36.
[82]Ibid., pp. 37f., 82.

preparatory schools, he wandered from job to job. New York producers refused his first major play, *The Zoo Story*. It reached Broadway in 1960. *The Death of Bessie Smith* opened in Berlin in 1960. *The American Dream* followed in 1961. But it was in 1962 that *Who's Afraid of Virginia Woolf?* became a sensational success.[83] Because of the success of its movie version, the play, *Who's Afraid of Virginia Woolf?*, has gained wide recognition. In this play the network of self-deceit, lies, and illusions is gradually and ruthlessly exposed. In modern terms, Albee has portrayed man as he is destroyed by his own acts. Later plays such as *Tiny Alice* (1964), *Malcolm* (1965), and *A Delicate Balance* (1966) have not been as successful or adequate.

Some critics contend that Albee would not have been so successful had it not been for the timing of his writing. By 1960, changed theatrical expectations cried out for a popular American playwright of "the Absurd." It was in this context that Albee became a culture hero almost immediately.[85]

It is true that Albee makes effective use of satire and comedy. He seeks to combine social protest with widely varying dramatic experimentation, and his work displays sensitivity to changing fashions and tastes.[86]

Tom Driver suggests that in his work Albee patches and stitches but does not follow through. Strong influences come from Beckett, Strindberg, Ionesco, and Pirandello. This material is used, however, in a rather clumsy and undigested way. For example, *Who's Afraid of Virginia Woolf?* is closely related to Strindberg's *Dance of Death* with "pop" mode and "camp" style adaptations. His flair for theatricalism, contends Driver, is not accompanied by adequate content and ability to organize. His works also display a tendency to cater, consciously or unconsciously, to a debased popular taste.[87] From

---

[83]Michael Rutenberg, *Edward Albee: Playwright in Protest* (New York: Drama Book Specialists Publications, Inc., 1969), pp. 3-7, and Nelvin Vos, *Eugene Ionesco and Edward Albee: a Critical Essay* (Grand Rapids, Mich.: William B. Eerdmans Publishing Co., 1968), pp. 45f.

[85]Driver, *Romantic Quest and Modern Theory*, p. 316.

[86]Rutenberg, *Edward Albee*, pp. 8-11.

[87]Driver, *Romantic Quest and Modern Theory*, pp. 317, 212.

a theological perspective, Wendell Harris has gone so far as to state that Albee denies all value systems whatever.[88]

The Frenchman, Henri Peyre, now professor of French at Yale, sees Beckett and Ionesco as prophets of dehumanization who reduce life to meaningless sound and fury. But ironically, for Peyre, the young people and professors of America have absorbed their works like one of those bitter and intoxicating drinks that make life appear exciting because it is replete with decay and senselessness. The academic critics and scholars of France are wary of them, while the scholars of England and America flock to them. Peyre asks the question, "Have they been magnified beyond their real stature or beyond what I believe one day will be the verdict of posterity?"[89] More puzzlement arises for a number of thoughtful people when it is noted that Beckett has recently been awarded the Nobel prize for literature.

With the dramatists of the Absurd, modern theater seems to have come to an end. The "Happening Theater" is not pure theater but a rebellion against theater. The "Happening" subordinates space to *occurrence*. In fulfilling itself, theater has exhausted itself and turned against itself.

Christian Responses to Post-Modern Literature and Drama

There is a negative quality about Post-Modern literature and drama which leaves the Christian dissatisfied and ill at ease. It is as if they bring us to a point of diagnosis, of painful analysis, and then leave us there.[90] The Classical-Moderns did not use orthodox Christian frames of doctrine, but at least they searched for some models to help men carry on and give significance to the human panorama. The Post-Moderns do not reflect the sacred and ultimate even in the negative and dialectical manner of Camus or Kafka. In these avant-garde writers there is an almost total lack of piety. There is a strange

---

[88]Wendell Harris, "Morality, Absurdity, and Albee," *Southwest Review*, XLIX. Summer, 1964, p. 250.

[89]Henri Peyre, *Modern Literature: The Literature of France* (Englewood Cliffs, N.J.: Prentice-Hall, Inc., 1966), p. 165.

[90]Whittle, *Christianity and the Arts*, p. 124.

new silence in this anti-teleological phase of literature and drama. It seems dry and unpromising. It would appear on the surface that there is little hope of communication between theology and the Post-Moderns.[91]

Men such as T. S. Eliot and Nathan Scott, however, would say that such a view is short-sighted. They see Post-Modern literature and drama as examples of Hunger-Art. There is always the possibility of there being an opening for grace as man reaches zero-point. There is the possibility of an opening for a radical new existence when, by some extreme crisis, the life of man is stripped of every secondary and false security. This stripping often compels men to submit to the cleansing processes of judgment and leaves them open for a rebuilding process on the basis of Christian structures.[92] In his last years, Dietrich Bonhoeffer said, "Now that it has come of age, the world is more godless, and perhaps it is for that reason nearer to God than ever before."[93] In other words, the godlessness of the Post-Moderns may point beyond itself to a fresh reintegration. Did not the "Death of God" theologians, such as Hamilton and Altizer, show their superficiality by their quickness to convert man's perplexity into a dogma about the "Death of God" and foreclose the possibility of renewal and reintegration?[94]

Perhaps God is preparing the way, after the absurd has turned us into the depths of the void, for a new day of blossoming. Theologians such as Gerhard Ebling and Heinrich Ott, for example, take this more positive approach. They would adopt and adapt the "later" Heidegger's emphasis that, although the No-More age of the gods has fled, there is the

---

[91]Scott, *Negative Capability,* pp. 49f. It is interesting to note that the Marxists also agree that there is a loss of a hierarchy of significance and the isolation of the individual from any significant relation to history in contemporary literature and drama. George Lukacs, the Marxist critic, suggests that Kafka, Proust, and Beckett reflect a destructive nihilism. Over against them he affirms that the new vision of the future should be a socialist realism exemplified by Brecht. Cf. Wilder, *The New Voice,* p. 180.

[92]Scott, *Craters of the Spirit,* p. 198.

[93]Dietrich Bonhoeffer, *Letters and Papers from Prison,* ed. Eberhard Bethge; trans. Reginald H. Fuller (London: SCM Press, Ltd., 1953), p. 167.

[94]Scott, *Negative Capability,* pp. 55f.

Not-Yet of the god that is coming.[95] Many feel that the "later" Heidegger can lead us part of the way, at least. He goes beyond the metaphors of the Post-Moderns such as nausea, the hole, viscosity, and the stare. Especially in his later writings, we encounter the metaphors of care, building, sojourning, dwelling, the open, homecoming, and logos.[96]

Heidegger has something like a historic Fall in his system. Before the Fall, there was a Golden Age when men submitted, abandoned, and surrendered themselves to what he calls Being.[97] Unfortunately, in the West, beginning with Plato, man sought to take over the universe and say that it is his own projection. Man soon came to regard the world as simply an image of man. The self cut itself off from the logos or roots of Being. Modern philosophy, since Kant, has preoccupied itself either with the thinking subject or with the object of thought and is skeptical of any attempt to find a unifying element.[98]

In contemporary life, according to Heidegger, the triumphs of scientific technology have been purchased by a "will to power" that has sundered our most elemental bonds with nature. We have such a manipulative approach to reality that all attentiveness to the weight and depth of Being is lost. We are fallen, inauthentic, and alien. We risk being devoured by the engines of our science and ideology. We must learn again the discipline of "letting-be"—of surrendering to the presence of Being.[99]

For Heidegger, the literary artists, especially poets such as Hölderlin and Rilke, are the instruments of the disclosure of the hiddenness of Being. The artist makes us look at the various concrete realities of lived experience and of history in a way that will permit them to disclose Ultimate Reality or Be-

---

[95]Martin Heidegger, *Existence and Being,* trans. by Douglas Scott, et al. (Chicago: Henry Regnery, 1949), p. 313.

[96]Stanley Romaine Hopper, "Literature—The Author in Search of His Anecdote," in *Restless Adventure,* ed. Roger L. Shinn (New York: Charles Scribner's Sons, 1968), p. 138.

[97]Martin Heidegger, *Being and Time,* trans. by John Macquarrie and E. S. Robinson (New York: Harper and Row, 1962), p. 220.

[98]Scott, *Negative Capability,* p. 65.

[99]Heidegger, *Being and Time,* pp. 183, 315-44. Cf. also Scott, *Negative Capability,* p. 66.

ing. *The artist thrusts us out to new levels of heightened perception where we experience the "shock of Being." A painter like Van Gogh can portray a pair of farm shoes in such a way that they vibrate with the silent call of earth. Van Gogh imparts "presence" to the shoes or a wheatfield or a starry night. In a world of gadgets, artifacts, and routines this vocation of the artist is urgent. According to Heidegger, we must return to the ultimate *power* of Being which guarantees to reality the character of permanence and stability and trustworthiness.[100]

As we have seen, language for the Post-Moderns, especially the Theater of the Absurd dramatists, is meaningless chatter. It becomes chatter because its source in the Logos is forgotten—it has fallen away from Being. The literary artist is the "Shepherd of Being." He must try to reunite language with Being. In the words of Hölderlin, there must be a "Homecoming."[101]

Some of the Post-Moderns wait as we have seen in Beckett's *Waiting for Godot*. John Dunne suggests that the theological uniqueness of Beckett's play, *Waiting for Godot,* is the possible depiction of the theme of "waiting for God." Although such an implication is denied by Beckett, his play has helped to act as a catalyst to accelerate extensive writing on the subject.[102] A careful analysis reveals that, for the Post-Moderns, there is no assurance that anyone will come, and if he does come that he will be gracious and helpful and have any specific intent.

For the Christian theologian, the greatest problem concerning Heidegger's vision is the character of Being that invites us, patiently and reverently, to await its advent. And how long must man wait? Can men live in a vacuum? The Post-Moderns have stripped us of old hopes and securities. What is next? The avant-garde dramatists have shown us our spiritual void. We have achieved in our time astonishing scientific and technical mastery. But, as Heidegger has pointed out, this mas-

---

[100]Ibid., pp. 232, 274-78, 387-88.
[101]Scott, *Negative Capability,* p. 70. Cf. also Hopper, "Literature," pp. 139-141.
[102]John S. Dunne, *A Search for God in Time and Memory* (New York: The Macmillan Company, 1969), p. 172.

tery has been purchased at the price of an exclusive attention to the world of objects. In this situation, it hardly seems possible for man seriously to concern himself with, or give himself to, that which transcends the finite order absolutely. It is ironical that precisely at that time when man has almost reached his goal of scientific and technical autonomy, his autonomy, his technology have made it possible for him to annihilate himself in an act of race-suicide. Gordon Kaufman asks if this is the beginning of the reign of the Anti-christ, which the early Christians taught was to precede the consummation of history (cf. II Thess. 2:3ff.).[103]

It is also ironic that the religions and art forms of the Far East, and their by-products, are coming to the West by Western invitation rather than by Eastern initiative. DeLubac has stated that the West is ripe for spiritual colonization. The dynamic and restless West cannot live in a spiritual vacuum.[104]

C. G. Jung, the influential psychologist, has admitted that his idea of the "Collective Unconsciousness" has Far Eastern roots. Timothy Leary has linked the L.S.D. experience with the *Tibetan Book of the Dead*. Francis Schaeffer contends that the basic reason why drugs are seen as a serious option is because man is desperate for meaning and "first-order" experiences.[105]

At this zero point in the history of the West, in this time of the spiritual vacuum, the theologian can agree with Heidegger that, although man is finite, he is unique and has a destiny. The Christian will go beyond Heidegger's view, however. Being is more than an impersonal principle. Rather, Being is personal and gracious and helpful and has specific historical intent.

The Christian theologian will point out, with John Macquarrie, that only some historical manifestation of Being, not fallen as man is fallen, can bring to man the concrete possi-

[103]Kaufman, *Systematic Theology*, p. 373.

[104]Hendrick Kraemer, *World Cultures and World Religions* (Philadelphia: Westminster Press, 1960), pp. 228-272.

[105]Francis A. Schaeffer, *Escape From Reason* (Chicago: Inter-Varsity Press, 1968), pp. 53-55.

bility of regaining authentic existence.[106] Such a power could not arrive immanently from the diseased and dying body described by the Post-Moderns. It would have to break into the historical order from beyond its bounds—from the Being, the personal God, who created not only man and his history, but all of the world.

The Christian faith, of course, holds that from the time of the Fall, when human history began its accelerating descent into perdition, God has been working to enter history with love and reconciliation. Finally, after long historical preparation, this became possible and actual in and with Jesus Christ. At the place of the Cross, man's human condition and basic problem was laid bare. God disclosed himself as a caring and suffering God as well as a holy Creator. In the Resurrection and the Coming of the Spirit, as well as the Cross, the New Age has arrived. The first fruits are available. The New Community is created and empowered to become the historical center from which reconciliation and healing flows. Nevertheless, the End is not yet. There is to be a final fulfillment, a consummation. At the end time—this rebellious history will be brought under the sovereignty of God.[107]

To describe the Christian view in more Heideggerian terms, Jesus reversed the process of fallenness. Jesus affirmed Being. He provided a primordial resurrection. Primordial Being is poured out through expressive Being into beings. The Son is the Logos or agent through which the Father creates and re-creates the world and beings in the world. The Holy Spirit is unitive Being for he unifies Being with the beings. This is not a Hegelian reabsorption. The Holy Spirit does not impose on man, but awakens and empowers him to the possibilities which he can either seize or let slip.[108]

Unfortunately, literary artists are often cut off (psychologically or otherwise) from most of the exciting and intensive

---

[106]John Macquarrie, *An Existentialist Theology* (London: SCM Press, 1955), p. 148.
[107]Kaufman, *Systematic Theology*, p. 377.
[108]John Macquarrie, *Principles of Christian Theology* (New York: Scribner's Sons, 1966), pp. 182, 246-250.

sources of theological enlightenment. The theologian, professional and lay alike, must take the initiative in removing misunderstandings about the nature of authentic Christianity. He must show that there is a third alternative to rigid and noncreative versions of Christianity *or* a despairing rebellion and absurdity.[109]

In one sense Heidegger is right, there is a waiting for a fuller Not-Yet. The early Christians believed that Jesus Christ had "inaugurated" but not completely fulfilled God's purposes. The Christian faith has an ontology of the "Not-Yet." Jurgen Moltmann has written about this "Not-Yet" in *Theology of Hope*.[110] A significant contribution of early Christianity was that it gave man a new quality of life oriented toward the future. In a world of fate and determinism, the early Christians shared this new way of hope. A tragedy of Christian history is that theologians have tended to become past-oriented. In the days ahead, the theologian must share with the creative people of the world the fact that the Christian community is not a community oriented just to the past, or to a transcendent world alone, but to the future. The Christian community seeks to reflect and change the world in the light of the model of the coming Kingdom of God, the New Jerusalem. Christians seek to be a flight ahead of the world, not a flight away from the world. The Christian community is more of a dynamic and flexible organism than an organization and a hierarchy. Christians gather to renew their vision and then scatter to share and serve and implement.[111]

---

[109]Kay Baxter, "Being and Faith in the Contemporary Theater" in *The Climate of Faith in Modern Literature,* ed. Nathan A. Scott, Jr. (New York: Seabury Press, 1964), p. 117. William F. Lynch, the prominent Roman Catholic critic, sees evidence for a counterrevolution in the arts. The *love* for alienation is beginning to ebb. Film audiences are becoming interested in the general questions about life. Lynch suggests that they do not want to be left in pure inwardness and nonrelation to reality or commitment. They want to get excited about the realities of freedom, anger, injustice and not just see them as art objects. Lynch sends out a call for film directors, painters and poets to help in the counterrevolution. Cf. William F. Lynch, "Counterrevolution in the Movies," in Cooper and Skrade, *Celluloid and Symbols,* pp. 111f., 121, 125.

[110]Jurgen Moltmann, *Theology of Hope,* trans. by James W. Leitch (Harper and Row, 1967).

[111]Carl E. Braaten, *The Future of God* (New York: Harper and Row, 1969), pp. 109-140.

The Post-Moderns in both literature and drama, as well as in the other arts, have revealed that man desperately needs a centralizing point of view so that life will not end in ridiculous absurdity. Nathan Scott describes this situation in the artistic world in a book appropriately entitled *The Broken Center.*[112] The zero point of chaos has been reached. It is time for the centralizing and empowering vision.

[112]Nathan A. Scott, Jr., *The Broken Center* (New Haven: Yale University Press, 1966), pp. 1-24.

THEOLOGY AND PAINTING

SINCE WORLD WAR I, we have witnessed the most staggering developments in the visual arts ever seen on this planet. In terms of quantity, momentum, initiation of the unique and influence in all areas of life, no other period of history comes close to matching recent art history.[1] This recent period, as well as the period between 1870 and 1918, and representative older painters, furnish important materials for a theological examination.

Theological categories will be utilized to evaluate painting in the last section of this discussion. A brief historical survey of the movement of art from the Classical, to the Classical-Modern, and then to the Post-Modern phases should provide a helpful background for the theological section.

Panorama of Contemporary Painting

The Classical approach claimed that a work of art was primarily an imitation or representation of nature. The painting

[1]Roger Ortmayer, "Art: Stages in the Act of Becoming," in *Restless Adventure,* ed. Roger L. Shinn (New York: Charles Scribner's Sons, 1968), pp. 180f. Cf. also Barbara Rose, *American Art Since 1900* (New York: Frederick A. Praeger, 1967).

told a story or gave an interpretation of an event or a person. The meaning of the painting was assumed to be identical with its content. "Good" paintings were neat and predictable and could be logically and objectively evaluated.[2]

IMPRESSIONISM AND CUBISM

The Impressionists, such as Monet, Renoir, and Pissarro, experimented with color as a light-reflecting agent. They moved their easels out-of-doors in order to approximate the reality of sunlight. Color was broken into minute areas and preserved on canvas. The pictures painted were only what their eyes really saw under specific conditions of light and shade.[3] The Cubists, including Braque, Leger, Duchamp, and the "early" Picasso, conducted an objective analysis of perspective, plane, and masses. They broke up and arbitrarily rearranged transparent planes and surfaces so that all sides could be seen at once. Although both of these groups gave us new ways of seeing things, they still saw art as an objective pursuit. They are Classical-Moderns.

EXPRESSIONISM

Expressionism is an umbrella term embracing related groups. These groups include the Post-Impressionists (Cézanne, Van Gogh, Gauguin), the "Brücke" group (Kirchner, Nolde), and the "Blue Rider" group (Kandinsky, Klee, Marc). The Expressionists are transitional. They began to break down the place of object and replace it with direct experience. Van Gogh transformed color into broken pigment. He allowed smashing rhythmic brushstrokes to reflect his own highly charged emotions and personal turbulence.[4] Kandinsky concentrated on the direct expression of emotional states through the interaction of color.[5] These painters utilized

[2]Ibid., p. 151.
[3]Katherine Kuh, *Break-up: The Core of Modern Art* (Greenwich, Conn.: New York Graphic Society, 1965), p. 11.
[4]Ibid.
[5]John W. Dixon, Jr., *Art As Communication* (Nashville: National Methodist Student Movement, 1957), p. 77.

pitted surfaces, broken outlines, unpredictable color, and scarred texture to intensify emotional expression. Rebellion and subjectivity were characteristics of these artists. Their poetic inward view of the self, however, was wedded to a real world outside.[6]

Thus they, too, can be called Classical-Moderns.

It also could be said that the non-representational art of Mondrian is in the same general category. He sought to bring painting into a consistent geometric and ordered relation.[7]

Post-Modern Emphases

Since World War II, dominant developments in painting have destroyed many elements of the Classical structure. For these Post-Moderns, paintings are seen as stages in the act of becoming. Logic has a minor role in the creation of art. The paintings tend to stretch to enormous size or they are only fragments. They are not dependent on a story or an event. The form of the painting is its content. Classical criticism is undercut. If the artist is asked about the meaning of a painting, he will often ask the viewer, "What does it mean to you?"[8]

A Classical painter usually works from sketches and preliminary drawings. Many of the Post-Moderns count on a spontaneous, sudden birth of painting activity. For some of these men, nothing is planned or conceptualized in advance. The very *act* of painting becomes the work of art.[9]

In view of these emphases, it is not surprising that little interest in academic art training is displayed by the Post-Moderns. Leaders such as Alan Kaprow, Claes Oldenburg, and Robert Whitman thumb their noses at the dominant Abstract Expressionists of the New York school. A painter such as Whitman is felt to be favored because he has no art school

---

[6]Ortmayer, "Art: Stages in the Act of Becoming," p. 173. Cf. also Sheldon Cheney, *Expressionism in Art* (New York: Liveright Publishing Corporation, 1958), pp. 69, 93f.

[7]William Gaunt, *Modern Art* (London: Frederick Warne & Co., Ltd., 1964), p. 55.

[8]Ortmayer, "Art: Stages in the Act of Becoming," p. 173.

[9]Ibid., p. 154.

training to unlearn.[10] Some of the artists turn to the circus to get ideas for "happenings." For them, the circus acts are composed with little consideration of logic and plot, and the acts make vivid and intense impressions.[11]

Mark Tobey, a prominent Post-Modern artist, states openly that he is out to smash the presanctified forms and constructions of official art. In fact, the Post-Moderns are calling into question all of the schemes of systematization, representation, and laws of beauty that have been built up through centuries of Western culture. In turn, they are seeking to replace them with images in dimensions, shapes, lines, and colors never before conceived.[12] Katherine Kuh has entitled her significant book *Break-Up: The Core of Modern Art*. She contends that recent art is characterized by shattered surfaces, broken color, segmented compositions, dissolving forms, and shredded images.[13]

DADAISM

One of the first frontal attacks on Classical forms was made by the Dadaists in the World War I period. Symbolically, the very word "Dada" (hobby-horse) was picked at random from a dictionary. Dada was a reaction to the horrors of the First World War, to the inhumanity and materialism of the modern world, and against the whole rationalistic tradition of Western thought and culture. It had no interest in art for art's sake, but was a cry for a change in the world. Leaders of the movement, such as Duchamp, Jean Arp, and Max Ernst, attempted to expose the snobbishness and pretentiousness of Classical art. To do this they utilized non-art subjects such as bicycle wheels, bottle holders, combs, and table utensils. They were anarchic, satirical, and ironic, and they opened the door for artistic freedom and invited spectator participation. They almost killed the pedantic term "Fine Arts." For them, the

[10]Ibid.
[11]Dore Ashton, "Major Directions in 20th Century Art," *The Church and the Visual Arts,* ed. Andrew J. Buehner (St. Louis, Mo.: Lutheran Academy for Scholarship, 1968), p. 16.
[12]Ortmayer, "Art: Stages in the Act of Becoming," p. 155f.
[13]Katherine Kuh, *Break-up: The Core of Modern Art,* p. 11.

boundaries between the various arts should be taken down and art should incorporate the element of play.[14]

Dada destroyed itself by its extremes. But to their credit is the emphasis that a painting is not just a thing to be seen or evaluated—it is an occurrence to be experienced.

SURREALISM

The Surrealists, such as Miró and Salvador Dali, went beyond the Dadaists and probed into "surreality" by investigating subconscious, spontaneous, and irrational configurations. Freud was a dominant influence in the movement which splintered time sequence and sought to recreate the disturbing life of our unconscious. In their struggle to escape the monotony of life, they turned to the irrational world of the subconscious.[15] Surrealism records feelings or thoughts normally thought to be outside the realm of expression, using symbols to convey the meanings of visual dreams. As a result, all sorts of fantastic and unreal forms appear in art.[16] It was a parallel movement to the "stream of consciousness" approach of James Joyce in literature. In fact, Surrealism is a mode of sensibility that cuts across all the arts in the twentieth century, including poetry, cinema, music, and even architecture. It destroys conventional meanings and creates new meanings or counter-meanings through radical juxtaposition (the collage principle). Surrealism stresses the extremes of disrelation, which is the subject of comedy. It seeks a higher reality in some deeper process of creativity, automatic composition, or visionary apocalypse.[17]

ABSTRACT EXPRESSIONISM

The Action painters or Abstract Expressionists, such as Jackson Pollock, de Kooning, Rothko, and Kline, have moved

---

[14]Ortmayer, "Art: Stages in the Act of Becoming," pp. 157f.
[15]Kuh, *Break-up,* pp. 12, 14.
[16]Milo Wold and Edmund Cykler, *Music and Art in the Western World* (Dubuque, Iowa: Wm. C. Brown Co., 1965), p. 246.
[17]Kuh, *Break-up,* pp. 12, 70, 105. Cf. also Susan Sontag, "Happenings," in *Against Interpretation,* pp. 269-298.

toward the experience of "creating" as being the work of art. For them, everything is shattered, including line, light, color, form, and pigment. They defy all rules as they reveal immediate spontaneous feelings. There is no one central idea but an incessant flow as the artist reports his impulsive and compulsive reactions. Franz Kline (1910-1962), for example, dashed on white and black lines with great spontaneity. Motherwell describes his work as a free improvisation, without any sketches or project in mind or, least of all, a model of any kind. In a playful way he calls it a higher form of doodling. He may discard a dozen such ventures and then something compelling breaks through to which he responds. Of course, Motherwell has had a life-long discipline as an artist. But he is detaching himself from older habits of seeing, so as to seek a fresh idiom as expression. In Jackson Pollock there is the final denial of all that Renaissance and Classical art stood for.[18]

POP ART

"Pop Art," as practiced by Larry Rivers, Oldenburg, Lichtenstein, Rosenquist, and Warhol, is a protest against some of the esoteric emphases of Abstract Expressionism. It utilizes the popular imagery of advertisement and objects of everyday life in a satirical way.[19] Pop Art is instantly to the point, extroverted rather than introverted.

Claes Oldenburg's work is intensely inner-directed. His work has been greatly affected by his environment. He changes as his environment changes. He has been involved in three main periods of work: "The Street," "The Store," and "The Home." In each case, he focuses on objects that we take for granted and by enlarging them shows us the depth of their meaning for our existence. The most significant art depiction is in the change of scale. Hamburgers are often as large as

---

[18]Cf. William Rubin, "Arshile Gorky, Surrealism, and the New American Painting," in *New York Painting and Sculpture: 1940–1970,* ed. Henry Geldzahler (New York: E. P. Dutton & Co., 1969), pp. 373-402. Cf. also Wilder, *The New Voice,* pp. 199f.

[19]Gaunt, *Modern Art,* p. 108. Cf. also Lucy R. Lippard, *Pop Art* (New York: Frederick A. Praeger, 1966), and Henry Geldzahler, *New York Painting and Sculpture: 1940–1970,* pp. 35-37.

beds. There are even monumental teddy bears that dwarf buildings. The art here represents an indictment of the "middle class" and its preoccupation with material things.[20] Perhaps the most intriguing implication of Pop Art is that it reflects the new American landscape—frenetic urban life. Turning away from form, Warhol portrays in a blatant way a soup can. He emphasizes that such a non-romanticized, non-gilded can is the real common stuff of twentieth-century experience.[21]

OP ART

Op Art is closely related to Kinetic art, for the effect is almost the same. It seems to assault the eye through interaction of color and images. Op Art, as practiced by Albers, Noland, Vasarely, and Clifford Still, is also experience and action art. It does have, however, some objective sense of order and precision. It creates a strong visual tension. The impression produced is one of violent kinetic movement. Uniform patterns are the rule of rectangles, squares, circles, and stripes. The response is primarily one of sensation.[22]

ASSEMBLAGE ART AND CONSTRUCTIVISM

Assemblage took its name from William C. Seitz's "Art of Assemblage" exposition in 1961. It has been said to be representative of the collage environment of neon signs, Broadway, commercials, and graveyards. Having its origins with Marcel Duchamp, it later was revived in the work of Johns and Rauschenburg. It has been described as collage with delusions of grandeur. The assemblage combines very different orders of existence and in this way it can create a type of poetic expression unlike any other art.[23]

---

[20]Neville Weston, *Kaleidoscope of Modern Art* (London: George G. Harrap and Co., 1968), p. 196. Cf. also Lippard, *Pop Art*, p. 11.

[21]Thomas Howard, *An Antique Drum* (Philadelphia: L. B. Lippincott Co., 1969), p. 91.

[22]Wendell Mathews, *The Christian Encounters the World of Painting* (St. Louis: Concordia, 1968), p. 82.

[23]Allan Kaprow, *Assemblage, Environments and Happenings* (New York: Harry N. Abrams, Inc., 1969), pp. 150-208.

Using materials related to industrial production, the new Constructivists, such as Grosvenor and Stella, use large constructions to define space.

KINETIC ART

Kinetic art, represented by Tinguely (1925—) and Schöffer (1912—), uses the wheels, sounds, and sights of the electronic age. David Medalla's work has exciting possibilities for movement and life in art. In his *Cloud Canyons,* continually running air pumps create a mixture of foam and water which pours out of a group of boxes of different heights. As the waters run, forms are endlessly created, assimilated or modified, and destroyed. The implications are fascinating: (1) it is a growing work of art—evolving from within and reacting to outside influences; (2) it exists only in the present —the work is always new; (3) it is random—it is free to do as it likes within the boundaries of the height of the box and the length of time the motor runs.[24] Kinetic art is man's attempt to create presence or life in contemporary art. Its implications for theology are far-reaching. Time has become a chief concern for the contemporary artist. And because of this concern, much Kinetic art represents movements of time. To visit a Kinetic gallery is to be intrigued by the wonder of moving light in its new formations. Larry Rivers comments that he uses electricity to make his visual projects light up and move even as Michelangelo used marble.[25]

Expo '67 in Montreal, Hemisfair in San Antonio, and Expo '70 in Japan suggest what is happening to art and art experience. Kaleidoscope, Labrynith, the Czech *Magica Laterna* (participation cinema), mosaic projections (polyvision), and wrap-around environmentals were featured.[26]

All of these developments call for participation both by the artist and the spectator. The "happening" was born. In fact,

---

[24]Guy Brett, *Kinetic Art: The Language of Movement* (New York: Reinhold Book Co., 1968), pp. 8–12.

[25]Roger Ortmayer, "The Art Work: Theological Understandings for Man's Aesthetic Ordering," *The Church and the Visual Arts,* ed. Andrew J. Buehner, pp. 153f.

[26]Ortmayer, "The Art Work," p. 155.

in some "happenings" enormous assemblages are actually destroyed by the artist and spectator.[27] Kaprow insists that artists are no longer producing monuments or heirlooms. This is why perishable materials are often used. Motherwell purposely makes paintings which disintegrate, much to the chagrin of collectors like Nelson Rockefeller. Rauschenberg mounted an electronic tennis game and had 500 members of the audience participate in a technological happening.[28]

The dominant emphasis, therefore, of Post-Modern art is that the object is secondary to the relationship experience. The aesthetic experience is seen as a three-way participation taking place in space and time between the artist, the spectator, and the object. Aesthetic experience is something that *happens*. One is actively and psychologically involved. It is not just something to be viewed.[29]

Implications for Contemporary Worship and Architecture

Before presenting an evaluation of Post-Modern painting, it will be helpful to show its implications for contemporary worship and architecture. In some ways, the new art is similar to participative worship in the early church. Avant-garde theologians are emphasizing that the new art can be seen as helpful in recovering a proper view of worship as participative celebration. They are pointing out that prayer has become festive-celebrative. To express gratitude and joy, Christian people are singing, dancing, and clapping hands. Post-industrial man is rediscovering festivity. There has been a recent eruption in the churches of multimedia services, jazz rituals, folk and rock worship services, and dance liturgies.[30]

At a recent national conference on Christian education, a "happening" was projected focused on the theme of "The Issue Is Change." It involved psychedelic imagination, new

[27]Ortmayer, "Art: Stages in the Act of Becoming," pp. 176f.
[28]Ashton, "Major Directions," p. 32.
[29]Ortmayer, "Art: Stages in the Act of Becoming," p. 177. Cf. also Allan Kaprow, *Assemblage, Environments and Happenings.*
[30]Cox, *Feast of Fools,* pp. 148, 48.

sounds, new rhythms, free form, and indeterminate sequences. As the 1300 people entered the room, they were greeted by colored lights and discordant sounds. Dancers acted out ideas such as "rejection." Members of the conference were soon involved—blowing balloons, throwing cardboard boxes in a pile, playing follow-the-leader and giving flowers to one another. Finally, after two hours of participation, they broke bread together, passing the loaves, pinching off pieces and singing, "Let us break bread together on our knees."[31]

Regardless of a person's reaction to this type of religious "happening," it must be said that authentic worship involves words, music, and movement in a simultaneous happening. Some of the new liturgies and celebrations may be seen as flashy gimmicks. Some are of slapdash quality, tasteless and boring. Furthermore, some Christian theologians distrust the body. Other theologians point out that the Incarnation is the way God revealed himself. The body in itself is not evil, they contend. Therefore, the return of rhythmic movement to the churches is being advocated by these theologians. Rhythmic movement is now being seen as literally thinking with the body. It is not just expressing through movement an idea or insight which is first thought in words or images. Joyous movement, radiant color, and piercing sound are now welcomed by many in churches as they seek to revitalize worship and stir the imagination. Jazz is seen as important because as a music form it encourages innovations and individual *ad libs* within a broad structure.[32]

Biblical theologians point out, however, that all Christian rituals must have both social and historical dimensions. Christianity utilizes symbol, but it is founded on specific historical events. It is anchored both in symbol, imagination, and fact. Multimedia experiences tend to suspend our classification ability, and sometimes new dimensions of awareness can be reached akin to the silent contemplation known by mystics. Of course, they can deteriorate into orgies. With delicacy

---

[31]Ortmayer, "The Art Work," pp. 149-151.
[32]Cox, *Feast of Fools*, pp. 49, 54, 52, 186, 162, 75.

and discipline, however, they can become occasions to lead us *into* historical existence and freedom. The Christian theologian is not against noise and revelry as such. He does ask that celebration go beyond the joy of the senses to the larger reality and the historical mission of which the Christian is a part.[33]

Real celebration links us to a world of memories, realities, values, and hopes that we share with the universal Christian community. In Christian festivals, historical events and concrete hopes are celebrated. Christianity has a definite bias for persons and events rather than for minds and ideas. Religious rebirth among young people is in a state of brawling turbulent infancy. It will have problems. The need is to embrace this spiritual renaissance without crushing it, enrich it without stifling it, and deepen it without mutilating it. It must be related to God's ongoing purpose.[34]

The Book of Revelation (Chapters 4 and 5) suggests that worship in the early church was noted as a time of celebration. Why should contemporary worship be mournful, sterile, and joyless? What about the utilization of guitars, harps, drums, and brass, as well as organs?[35]

Exciting new buildings are now being planned for such flexible and dynamic worship. If the church building is multipurpose, as many advocate, it should be constructed so that it can be adjusted to be distinctive in an emotional and psychological sense. Moveable elements may be used which could be adjusted to different space requirements. The environment could be formed by light-sound produced by projections and electronic music. Films, slide mixtures, and overhead color projections may be used. The congregation could better be brought into physical participation with a proper setting. The liturgy should be seen as environment—auditory, visual, and tactile as well as verbal. The function of the liturgy and architecture would determine the form. For

[33]Ibid., pp. 73, 79, 80, 109f.
[34]Ibid., pp. 110–112.
[35]Howard Moody, "Worship as Celebration and Confrontation" in *Multi-Media Worship,* ed. Myron B. Bloy, Jr. (New York: Seabury Press, 1969), p. 93.

example, architecture could encourage a person to participate rather than be a spectator.[36]

Many suggest that the church-room should not be isolated but should stand in the middle of the "profane" activities of city life. Is the best place for worship a place set aside as a "sanctuary" or a place made holy by human happenings of many kinds? Should the place of meeting be a non-directional room of festive character?[37] The emphasis would be on process, relationship, and presence and not just on objective content or universal ideas. Have we been too highly rational and verbal in our services? Is McLuhan right when he says that we have moved into the dynamics of the "image age"? Is our language of worship too archaic and stilted?

The biblical emphasis suggests that Christ communicates himself through the actual participation of the people in worship and involvement in his dynamic and ongoing redemptive purpose. Is James F. White correct in entitling his book on worship *The Worldliness of Worship?*[38] Is Erik Routley right when he says that worship is drama?[39]

The Post-Moderns have much to teach us. Celebration and "happenings" are important as long as we follow the Christian guidelines about *how* we celebrate. There is a Christian *style* of celebration.[40] Amos censured fertility rites. Paul criticized glossolalia groups and the "spirituals" at Corinth and gave guidelines for worship.

Evaluation of Post-Modern Painting

The study of the wider implications of Post-Modern painting

---

[36]Cf. privately circulated papers: Justus Dahinden, "Church of the Future," and Roger Ortmayer, "Liturgy, Environment, Form and Faith."

[37]Lothar Kallmeyer, "New Tendencies in Protestant Church Building" in *Revolution, Place, and Symbol*, ed. R. L. Hunt (New York: International Congress on Religion, Architecture and the Visual Arts, 1969), p. 186.

[38]James F. White, *The Worldliness of Worship* (New York: Oxford University Press, 1967).

[39]Erik Routley, *Words, Music and the Church* (New York: Abingdon Press, 1968), pp. 129–131.

[40]Ortmayer, "The Art Work," pp. 159f. Cf. also F. Debuyst, *Modern Architecture and Christian Celebration* (Richmond, Va.: John Knox Press, 1968).

should provide a broader perspective for its evaluation. Despite the salutary emphases of the Post-Moderns, there are problems in some of their tenets for those who seek to follow biblical guidelines. Post-Modern art has little relation to any truth or absolute external to itself. In fact, most of the Post-Moderns do not give their pictures any names or designations other than numbers. If names are given, they usually are applied some time after the painting has been finished. Mark Rothko distinguishes his canvases by color, *Black over Red* or *Light Earth and Blue*.[41] Joseph Sittler suggests that contemporary painting seems to be a nonverbal wrestling with a shifting sensibility. It is a probing-for-the-possible in a wilderness.[42]

Action painters, such as Pollock, Kline, and Gorky, create from nothing. From a theological perspective, such activity is reserved only for God. Gorky did commit suicide. Pollock's fast driving on narrow, crooked roads asked for death—which came in a wreck.[43]

Seen in perspective, each of the groups mentioned—Classical, Classical-Modern, and Post-Modern—have some valid insights. Artists do imitate, and they do express subjective emotions. The artist also is a constructor of material into a structured form. In fact, a work of art is composed of matter and content as well as form. Of great importance in the work of an artist is his material with its particular qualities. Form is the shape that results from the creative, making aspect of the artist's work. Content in the visual arts cannot be translated into words nor is there any verbal equivalent of artistic content. Thus, the understanding of paintings requires the spectator to enter a world which has its own structures and its own laws.[44] Painters talk with line, shape, color, texture, and space. Gauguin states that a straight line suggests the infinite and a curved line suggests creation. Certain color harmonies are peaceful and others are exciting. Artists, above all, strive

---

[41]Ortmayer, "The Art Work," p. 163. Cf. also Roy McMullen, *Art, Affluence, and Alienation* (London: Pall Mall Press, 1968), pp. 139–160.

[42]Joseph Sittler, "The Theological Situation: The Achievement of Values in Architecture," in *Revolution, Place, and Symbol*, pp. 22f.

[43]Ortmayer, "The Art Work," p. 165.

[44]Dixon, *Nature and Grace in Art*, pp. 63f, 105f.

for fresh and individual statements. That which is added to or said about the human experience is "content."[45]

As was noted in the historical survey, the ways in which artists set forth their apprehensions of reality are extremely varied. The Realist tradition is still powerful. Realism has always appeared whenever a purgative force has been needed to clear away a style which has become too self-conscious. A modern super-Realist like Andrew Wyeth focuses the attention on a subject so acutely that we are forced to see it in a new way. A notable example is his 1948 painting entitled *Christina's World*. Much Abstract painting delights in the materials and their combination and relationship and is natural in this sense. And some Expressionistic artists seek not so much to see and analyze, but to feel and react.[46]

What is the response to these developments of a person who seeks to live under the guidance of biblical guidelines? Already we have seen the value of the Post-Modern emphasis on subjective commitment and new relationships in contrast to abstract knowledge. On the other hand, we have noted that God is an objective personal reality (the God who is there) and has revealed himself concretely and historically. There are broad revealed principles and realities available to guide or focalize action and commitment.

Theological Categories for Evaluation

Another type of response for the theologian is to seek to develop an art correlation and criticism based on Christian categories. It is granted that these categories will have a limited acceptability beyond the Christian community. Such a correlation and criticism, however, will help to give the Christian a needed perspective with which to view the chaotic field of painting. The various schools of art and representative

---

[45]Jean Mary Morman, *Art: of Wonder and a World* (New York: Art Education, Inc., 1967), pp. 18f. Cf. also Jerrold Morris, *On the Enjoyment of Modern Art* (Greenwich, Conn.: New York Graphic Society, 1968), pp. 26–34.
[46]Morris, *On the Enjoyment of Modern Art*, pp. 47f.

individual artists will be considered in terms of four basic theological categories: The arts of creation, of man in the image of God, of the fall, and of redemption.[47] For the sake of perspective, some non-contemporary artists will be discussed.[48]

The Arts of Creation

Both the world and man are seen by the Christian vision as created by God. Man is placed in creation, for one thing, to rejoice in it. By nature man is finite and sinful. In the final

[47]Dixon, *Nature and Grace in Art,* p. 72.

[48]For reproductions of the pictures referred to in this study and general discussion of the painters, consult any good history of painting. Especially helpful to the author have been the following books:

Werner Haftmann, *Painting in the Twentieth Century* (New York: Frederick A. Praeger, 1961). Volumes I and II.

Neville Weston, *Kaleidoscope of Modern Art* (London: George G. Harrap & Co., 1968).

Alfred H. Barr, Jr., *Masters of Modern Art* (New York: The Museum of Modern Art, 1958).

Emile Langui, *50 Years of Modern Art* (New York: Frederick A. Praeger, 1959).

William Fleming, *Arts and Ideas* (New York: Henry Holt and Company, 1955).

Helen Gardner, *Art Through the Ages* (New York: Harcourt, Brace, and Company, 1948).

E. H. Gombrich, *The Story of Art* (New York: Phaidon Publishers Inc., 1960).

John Canady, *Mainstreams of Modern Art* (New York: Simon and Schuster, 1959).

H. W. Janson and Dora Jane Janson, *The Picture History of Painting* (New York: Harry N. Abrams, Inc., 1957).

Sarah Newmeyer, *Enjoying Modern Art* (New York: The New American Library of World Literature, Inc., 1955).

Erwin O. Christensen, *The History of Western Art* (New York: The New American Library of World Literature, Inc., 1959).

Rene Huyghe, ed., *Larousse Encyclopedia of Modern Art* (New York: Prometheus Press, 1965).

New York: the New Art Scene (New York: Holt, Rinehart and Winston, 1967).

Joseph-Emile Muller, *Modern Painting* (New York: Castle Books, 1960).

Please note the specialized books on specific schools of painting in the footnotes.

Colored slides can be obtained from the American Library Color Slide Co., 222 West 23rd St., New York City; Contemporary Slides, 243 East 17th St., New York.

Reproductions are available at Metropolitan Museum of Art, New York City; Museum of Modern Art, 11 West 53rd, New York City: and National Gallery of Art, Wash., D.C.

sense, he can only see creation through his finiteness and his sinfulness. However, in the arts, it is possible for man to come closer to the purity of nature, for example, than he can in any other activity.[49]

MONET

An authentic artist's work is subservient in a large degree to his material. This means that he will usually stay rather close to the freshness of nature if he is painting nature. Oftentimes he is able to cultivate the innocence and directness of vision that are associated with unfallen nature.[50] Mozart has something of this quality in music. Monet's (1840-1926) pictures, such as *La Grenouillère,* give us a fresh impression of nature. Monet showed how light, in its multiple aspects, changed landscapes. This reproduction of realistic sunlight brought a new luminosity to nature.[51]

VAN GOGH

Naturalism only becomes a religious work, however, when it embodies awe beyond the immediately physical. Vincent van Gogh (1853-1890) had something of this ability to express the dimension of depth in encountered reality. In *Starry Night* there seems to be a triumph of the spirit over a narrowly scientific view of the world. In order to achieve this effect, he used violent colors, broken pigment, crude forms, and restless rhythms. It is close to the Hebraic emphasis. Nature and earth seem to be alive, united by the dynamic flow of cosmic energy.[52]

Disappointed in his attempts at serving God as a missionary in a poor Belgian mining district, Van Gogh poured out his spiritual hunger in painting. He painted few specifically religious pictures, but his paintings, such as *Wheatfield* and *Garden in Arles,* speak of his sense of holy awe.

---

[49]Dixon, *Nature and Grace in Art,* p. 71.
[50]Ibid., p. 71ff.
[51]Kuh, *Break-up,* p. 18.
[52]Alfred H. Barr, Jr., *What is Modern Painting?* (New York: The Museum of Modern Art, 1956), p. 18f.

ACTION PAINTERS AND POLLOCK

From one perspective, Action painters can be seen as performing the arts of creation. Many of them have delight in the art of making, in bringing into existence a structure that had not been in existence before. Some artists, such as Kline, use their canvases as instruments of self-revelation. Others, such as Rothko, create more of a total image. Some critics see design in Pollock's drippings. Barnett Newman fills large canvases with a single color interrupted only occasionally by vertical stripes. In his freedom from distraction and diversion some see a mystical religious emphasis. The mystics often suggested that one should approach the divine only by successive emptyings of oneself.[53]

On the other hand, Jackson Pollock's (1912-1956) later work can be seen as an example of what has happened in our culture with the loss of the sense of God's presence in creation. Pollock is an Action painter or an Abstract Expressionist. His *Number 1* exhibits a feverish mood of crisis and a fierce sense of nihilism. His painting was an intangible flow without prearranged content and form. No one before or since has dared to ignore so completely all established rules. He uses dense swirling webs, drips, dribbles, and tangles of paint. It is a sensory record of his own feelings about his surroundings. He created a fury to escape the fury within himself.[54] In an interview, Pollock suggests that he has given up objective data and recognizable form because the contemporary age is an age of indeterminacy. It is impossible to paint like Rembrandt in an age of fragmented forms and atomic destruction.[55] The painting is without a center or horizon. The result is a sense of vertigo and an overwhelming sense of God's absence.

---

[53]Thomas F. Mathews, "The Problem of Religious Content in Contemporary Art," in *Revolution, Place and Symbol*, pp. 122, 123, 126.

[54]Kuh, *Break-up*, p. 105.

[55]Seldon Rodman, *Conversations with Artists* (New York: Capricorn Books, 1961), p. 83.

WARHOL

In reaction to the abstractions of men like Pollock, Andy Warhol has turned away from all form and confronts us with the brutal concrete facts of our twentieth century in the form of a plain *Soup Can*. "Pop" art confronts us simply with the presence of the object in all its self-assertiveness. Warhol wants us to see with a fresh eye objects which we have not noticed because of familiarity.[56]

The Arts of Man in the Image of God

According to the Genesis narrative, man is appointed to have dominion over the earth and to subdue it. Art is not to be an instrument of his lust, but rather should be used to exhibit things as they are in their inherent nature. Man is to understand, order, tend, and use creation. In the arts he probes and tests. He imposes order and seeks to give man grasp and dominion over creation. This type of art is an intellectual art which is often colder in effect. This art of exploration and analysis is the art of man in the image of God.[57]

PIERO DELLA FRANCESCA

Piero della Francesca, the fifteenth-century Italian painter, sees the order of things as part of the incarnated Holy. His art is mathematical. In his *Resurrection* there is pure presentation in geometrical form and cool harmony. This painting shows Christ as he steps forth from the tomb, the flag of victory in his hand.[58]

Piero's passion for geometry, as form and symbol, explains the design of the base of the tomb and the head of Christ in an isosceles triangle. At its apex Piero painted the most powerful head of Christ of the entire fifteenth century.

---

[56]Mathews, "The Problem," pp. 120f.
[57]Dixon, *Nature and Grace in Art*, p. 74.
[58]Walter L. Nathan, *Art and the Message of the Church* (Philadelphia: The Westminster Press, 1961), p. 78.

Through the eyes, Piero conveys the concept of the risen Christ awakening into a world beyond mortal vision. The rigidity of his face and pose, and his obliviousness to his surroundings suggest a spiritual or psychological rather than physical transformation. True to the account of the resurrection, Piero shows Christ in human form. His body still has material weight, as seen by the pressure of his leg on the tomb's edge. The dark areas around the eyes speak of the passion and the long entombment.

The landscape to Christ's right is one of winter, and like the wound in his right side, indicative of death. To Christ's left is the springtime of nature, alive and verdant through his sacrifice. Thus the landscape signifies the world before and after his Coming. In the paintings of Piero which show Christ before death, he is a submissive gentle figure. Resurrected, he is a masculine militant being.

PICASSO AND BRAQUE

Cubism is not primarily an art showing the brokenness of the world. With Cézanne and other Cubists who followed his leadership, man was freed from the tyranny of the object. In its later stages, Cubism was often witty and playful.[59] Cubism is pure construction that makes allusion to recognizable objects for a structural purpose only. This is seen in Picasso's *Man with a Pipe*. It shows man's control over the object. Braque (1882-1963), another Cubist, in *Man with a Guitar* breaks up forms into an almost non-recognizable pattern but then rearranges them and superimposes them on each other.[60]

MONDRIAN

Piet Mondrian (1872-1944) is the strictest and most "architectural" of all abstract painters. His pictures are composed entirely of solid squares or rectangles, and all the lines have to go either straight up and down or across. His effort was

---

[59]Dixon, *Nature and Grace in Art,* pp. 188f.
[60]Kuh, *Break-up,* p. 41.

directed toward order and clarity. It would seem that a language with such a small "vocabulary" could not possibly say a great deal. His painting proves, however, that this need not be true at all. Mondrian's art has a spine-tingling liveliness. The entire design of *Broadway Boogie Woogie,* a later picture, moves with the pulse beat of the big city with its flashing neon signs and its stop-and-go traffic along precisely laid-out patterns. Color, line, and proportion are tightly balanced, producing harmony. His original arrangements of pure space show the power of an artist to influence design and human thinking. He felt that his art of harmony would help resolve conflicts and reflect the cosmic order.[61]

Another painter who could be included in the category of man made in the image of God is Paul Klee, who with his touch of fantasy, discovery, and humor is fresh and creative. Marc Chagall, likewise, is creative, sentimental, and mysterious.[62]

The Arts of the Fall

The biblical drama pictures man as fallen and as having sinned against God in his lust and in his pride. Thus man has broken the goodness of his relation to reality. An artist, as a person of sensitivity, is especially aware of the brokenness of man and the world. He penetrates into the tragedy of existence and investigates the nature or consequence of the Fall. Fallen existence itself or the kind of world that results from the Fall is also investigated. Such seeing and concern combined with portrayal comprise the arts of the Fall.[63]

As a human enterprise, art must manifest the brokenness of the world and the rebellion of man. Unfortunately, some art exploits man's lust and is used as an instrument of man's self-assertion, arrogance, power, and passion. However, an

---

[61]Werner Haftmann, *Painting in the Twentieth Century, Volume One* (New York: Frederick A. Praeger, 1965), pp. 200–203.
[62]George A. Flanagan, *How to Understand Modern Art* (New York: Thomas Y. Crowell Co., 1962), pp. 256, 260.
[63]Dixon, *Nature and Grace in Art,* pp. 70f.

authentic artist, even if he is not personally moral, stays with the integrity of his material.[64]

DALI

The development in psychiatry which emphasized that man's subconscious is important in regard to human behavior influenced painting. Artists were immediately intrigued by the field of psychiatry and began to explore the possibilities of metaphysical expression in Surrealist painting. In these paintings, dreams were given figuration and the subconscious was plumbed for images. In Surrealism the objects are torn loose from their natural context and used to construct a new world under the will and imagination of the artist. Salvador Dali's (1904—) picture entitled *Persistence of Memory* reflects the subconscious, the dreams of that world discovered by Freud.[65] With its limp watches, it is an unforgettable painting. His sense of space becomes limitless by the elimination of atmosphere and by making the distant objects as detailed as the closer ones. The dead fish and the crawling ants are symbolic of the infinity of time itself.

MUNCH

It is the Expressionists who find their special concern in the passions, cruelty, and despair of man trapped in his human dilemma. Existentialists and theologians like Paul Tillich value the Expressionists highly. Paintings that are valued include the demon-ridden horror of the works of Munch (1863-1944). A Scandinavian Expressionist, Munch was a high-strung, sensitive painter of the gruesome and morbid: women embracing skeletons, funerals, sickness, and fear. This is not art to be enjoyed or simply to serve as decoration; it is a means of exteriorizing the artist's sense of the contradictory, gloomy torment of life.

---

[64]Ibid., pp. 75f.
[65]Barr, *What is Modern Painting?* Cf. also William S. Rubin, *Dada, Surrealism, and Their Heritage* (New York: Museum of Modern Art, 1968), pp. 109–113.

In such pictures as *The Scream* or *The Cry,* Munch presents in an unforgettable way some of man's basic problems. Especially notable are the looming contours and sweeping brush strokes. Loneliness, frozen fear, and anxiety are vividly portrayed. In the distance is a harbor. The sky above is ominous with angry red clouds. The female figure is uttering her terrible cry. He uses opposing ribbons of black to isolate her ghost-like face and set up tensions.

Munch's mother died when he was five. His father lived in morbid anguish. In a picture like *The Cry,* Munch portrays his own basic problem and in turn helps others to face up to their own problems.[66]

PICASSO

Picasso's (1881—) *Girl Before A Mirror* and *Guernica* are other examples of Expressionist paintings. Picasso is the master painter who has utilized or inaugurated most of the modern kinds of painting. He passed through his "Blue Period" to the "Pink Period." During his "Cubist Period," he portrayed man's condition in a powerful way. The picture *Girl Before A Mirror* is a synthetic Cubist picture. Here Picasso cuts up the girl and then asserts his independence in his reassembling of the parts. Picasso presents the girl from different points of view simultaneously. He has reflected the recent scientific discoveries in the field of time-space relations by destroying the traditional sense of time and space. He has superimposed a profile view on a frontal view of the face and then reflects the image in the mirror.[67] Looking at this picture is like facing a psychiatrist. It shows a person that he, also, is loaded with all kinds of problems, guilt, and mischief. It is a shocking picture painted in 1932 by the master.

One prominent leader has called Picasso's *Guernica* the greatest truly Protestant painting. I have studied this picture many times in the Museum of Modern Art in New York City,

---

[66]George W. Digby, *Meaning and Symbol* (London: Faber and Faber 1955), pp. 29–39. Cf. also Otto Benesch, *Edvard Munch* (Garden City, New York: Phaidon Co., 1960).

[67]Wold and Cykler, *Music and Art*, p. 271.

and it always has a very moving effect on me. Guernica was
a small city in Northern Spain. Here the Fascist countries,
Germany and Italy, helped the Fascist Spaniards to overthrow
the Loyalist government, the official government in 1937. This
small town was completely destroyed by an air attack by the
Italians and Germans—the first saturation bombing. One
thousand people were killed. Two days later Picasso took
his revenge against Franco who was the Fascist leader. He
began this twenty-six foot mural for the Spanish building at the
Paris World's Fair.[68]

Picasso states that *Guernica* symbolizes brutality and
darkness. In the picture a woman is portrayed with her
clothes on fire, falling and shrieking from a burning house.
Another woman rushes in toward the center of the picture
with her arms flung wide in despair. A powerful portrayal is made of a dying horse sinking to his knees, his
screaming head flung back. Picasso uses only black, white,
and gray—the grim colors of mourning. If modern art means
that we should not cover up anything but rather look at the
human situation in the depth of its estrangement, guilt, and
despair, then in this negative way *Guernica* is one of the
most powerful pictures ever painted.[69]

OROZCO

In 1922 a group of young Mexican painters formed an
artists' syndicate and revived the almost extinct technique of
fresco painting. They hoped to create a new monumental
art that would speak to the people. Among the most important of these artists was Orozco. Orozco's *Catharsis* or
Struggle is tragic in its emphasis—portraying the fact that
man has been exploited and brutalized. Various symbols of
greed and war are painted in vivid colors. A woman with a

---

[68]Paul Tillich, "Existentialist Aspects of Modern Art" in *Christianity and
the Existentialists,* ed. Carl Michalson (New York: Scribner's, 1956), pp.
137f.
[69]Kuh, *Break-up,* pp. 65f. Cf. also Jane Dillenberger, *Secular Art with
Sacred Themes* (New York: Abingdon Press, 1969), p. 98.

gold tooth and distorted figure symbolizes moral decay.[70] It may be seen in the Palace of Fine Arts in Mexico City.

ROUAULT

Very few artists see beyond the tragedy to the redemption. Rouault is an exception. Rouault, however, also had the capacity for passionate protest against conditions which degrade men and women. His picture entitled *The Prostitutes* is an example. A professor of art in New Mexico recounts that he was quite disgusted when he first visited an exhibition of the paintings of Rouault which pictured dissipated French magistrates and prostitutes. He was leaving the gallery when he noticed the guided tour starting out. Joining it, he heard the lecturer say that Rouault was a deeply religious man whose paintings represented the disgust and loathing he felt for evil things, especially those evils symbolized by prostitutes and by the world's repudiation of Christ. This professor then realized that he had misunderstood the artist and failed to comprehend what he was saying.[71]

DE KOONING

De Kooning's (1904—) *Woman, No. 1* could well be included in the arts of tragedy. Dutch-born Willem de Kooning is an American painter whose art has helped make New York the center of new developments in painting. In his *Woman, No. 1*, the first of savage series, the woman seems to be all eyes, teeth, and breasts. "I didn't mean to make them such monsters," he affirmed. And on another occasion he said, "Women irritate me sometimes. I painted that irritation in the Woman series, that's all." The anatomy of *Woman, No. 1* is ambiguous: a neck and a thumb change places; a knee or a shoulder is salvaged from the chaos of paint just

[70]*Motive*, November, 1960, p. 16. Cf. *Jose Clemente Orozco, An Autobiography* (Austin, Texas: University of Texas Press, 1962).
[71]Clyde S. Kilby, *Christianity and Aesthetics* (Chicago: Inter-Varsity Press, 1969), p. 37.

before it vanishes altogether. Letters and numbers are often introduced to create the double illusion of meaning and meaninglessness. Usually rejecting preliminary sketches, de Kooning allows his own urgent feelings to guide him. The woman's form has the appearance of compulsive magic. Only the eyes and mouth have clarity. The "Pop" aspects of Hollywood glamour are missing.[72]

A painter friend once remarked that she found de Kooning's women too personal and too terrible to endure. Here is the human image depicted with a sense of horror and brutality, of tragedy and hopelessness. Yet at the same time the horror of these images is lightened by a sense of comedy; these are the cheerful guys and dolls of Hollywood, the cheese-cake goddesses of the American billboard. Are de Kooning's figures satirical or pathetic? When an artist makes his work an instrument of his lust, it is pornography. De Kooning would not be in the category of pornography.

GORKY

Some modern Abstract Expressionists such as Gorky and Rothko reflect the arts of the Fall. Not an Action painter like Pollock, Gorky (1904-48) might be called an Abstract Surrealist. Gorky's art is accompanied by a sense of agony and nausea. Gorky is to painting what Dostoevsky is to literature —the explorer and uncoverer of a new psychological space. The beautiful and tragic painting, *Agony* (1947), suggests an interior context. Its lines and shapes—part animal, part mechanical—form a fearful specter, a primitive fetish. The grays and running pools of black speak of anxiety and despair. The cold yellows speak of nausea, and the smoldering and feverish reds speak of an internal fire which burns without destroying. Incoherence and meaninglessness, solitude and despair, are the chief characteristics of Gorky's art. His also is the truth of the void, of the end.[73]

Gorky's art reflected an unbelievable string of tragedies that

---

[72]Kuh, *Break-up,* p. 73 and Weston, *Kaleidoscope,* p. 205.
[73]Weston, *Kaleidoscope,* p. 204.

led to his suicide in 1948. A fire destroyed his studio and much of his work. This disaster was coupled with personal problems and troubles such as cancer, sexual impotence, and a broken neck. His last pictures reflected these personal problems and were marked by extremes of pathos and aggression.[74]

WOOD

Grant Wood's *Daughters of Revolution* reveals pride. This painting is ruthless in its demolition of pompousness and pride. Especially noteworthy are the exact close-up details of the picture, including the eyes of the women, the prim lace collars, the hand with the colonial teacup, and the yellowed patriotic engraving. All of this reinforces the disquieting effect of the virtuous tight-lipped faces.[75] Wood's picture reminds us of the way in which Faulkner criticizes religious people in his writings such as *The Sound and the Fury*.

The sense of the void of man's alienation from man and God, of cruelty and despair are a special concern to the Christian. He has a different view, however, from the writer of classical tragedy or the painter of contemporary tragedy. The Christian sees tragedy not as the end of man, but as a rent in the wholeness of creation, the consequence of sin and revolt. There is also hope beyond the tragedy.[76]

The Arts of Redemption

Another emphasis of the biblical drama is that God is involved in a redemptive process, seeking to transform the old into a new creation and thus to transfigure the relation of man to reality and himself.[77] This final category belongs to Christians alone, for redemption is an act of God that is not generally apprehended except under the grace cf God. The holiness of Christ seeks to penetrate the material world and bring into being the new earth. A special delight in crea-

---

[74]Rubin, *Dada, Surrealism*, pp. 173f.
[75]Haftmann, *Painting in the Twentieth Century*, Vol. I, pp. 298f.
[76]Dixon, *Nature and Grace in Art*, p. 199.
[77]Ibid., p. 80.

tion comes through Christ who opens a person's eyes and purifies his soul. This art is informed by a glory transfigured out of pain. Tragedy here has been redeemed and transformed, not obliterated or forgotten, but caught up in a new meaning and a new life.[78]

Man cannot make a redemptive art, but he can make an art that communicates what he experiences of redemption as a man and what he knows of it as an artist. Only God is the Redeemer. This art encompasses the great Christian tensions such as sin and holiness, tragedy and triumph.[79]

GRÜNEWALD

Grünewald's masterpiece, the *Isenheim Altarpiece,* was painted just about the time Michelangelo finished the Sistine ceiling. Grünewald seems obsessed with the tragedy of man. In his *Crucifixion* he has caught the somber aspect of the cross. This Christ is both God and man; never have the agonies of his flesh been more starkly revealed, yet his great size is far beyond human scale.[80]

Another of the significant pictures by Grünewald is *The Resurrection.* The radiance which surrounds the figure of Christ in this painting has a mystical quality which is Expressionistic rather than Naturalistic, but it is never merely beautiful. In this picture Christ does not merely rise from the grave, but he explodes upward in a spiraling rush, still trailing his shroud and shining with a light as brilliant as the sun against the midnight sky. The guardians of the tomb, the forces of death, blindly grope along the ground in utter defeat. Here the strange genius of Grünewald has created its most unforgettable image.[81]

The halo, larger and more brilliant than any other in the history of European painting, not only surrounds the risen

---

[78]Ibid., pp. 71, 199.
[79]Ibid., p. 78.
[80]Nathan, *Art and the Message of the Church,* p. 78. Cf. also Jane Dillenberger, *Style and Content in Christian Art* (New York: Abingdon Press, 1965), pp. 143–149.
[81]J. K. Huysmans, *Grünewald* (Garden City, New York: Phaidon Press, 1958), pp. 8f.

Christ with its colored light, it even penetrates his flesh, setting it afire, as it were, and thus changing it from a material substance into a thing transfigured and purified. Before our very eyes, Grünewald causes the Christ who suffered as a man to become a heavenly being.[82]

REMBRANDT

Rembrandt was born in Leyden, Holland (1606), the son of a miller. He was a man full of passion and power with the gift of being able to express with his brush most, if not all, of what the human heart can feel. In his soul lived the deepest reverence for the spiritual potentialities of art that has appeared in the world since Michelangelo.

John Dixon maintains that more than any other individual artist, Rembrandt comes to the events of the Christian faith in their biblical record with no preconceptions. As much as an artist can, he responded to the reality of the biblical events directly with the materials and forms of his art.[83]

In the midst of Rembrandt's career, a radical change in the circumstances of his life and his introduction to the Bible resulted in the development of a new style. This transformation is particularly evident in his etchings on biblical themes. No longer did he present Christ in terms of earthly power and Baroque magnificence. He had learned the biblical and Reformation understanding that God's disclosure in the Christ has a hidden quality. Thus Rembrandt acquired a style which was suitable to convey his new understanding of religious truth. Thereafter, he presented the Christ in such terms of simplicity and humility that only by faith and through faith could one recognize in this ordinary man the Christ of God.[84]

In Rembrandt's best-known *Head of Christ* is seen a

---

[82]Ibid.

[83]Dixon, *Nature and Grace in Art*, p. 162.

[84]M. P. Halverson, "What is Art? When is it Christian?" *International Journal of Religious Education*, Vol. 35, No. 6 (February, 1959), p. 13. Cf. also Franz Landsberger, *Rembrandt, The Jews and the Bible* (Philadelphia: The Jewish Publication Society of America, 1961), and W. A. Visser 'T Hooft, *Rembrandt and the Gospel* (Philadelphia: The Westminster Press, 1957).

warmth and depth of feeling seldom found. The light comes from within the figure rather than from without. There is a subtle contrast in the face—on the left side is sadness but the right cheek is ruddy. The nose and chin are strong but parted lips seem to speak with tenderness. The brow is dented by thought. The large, thoughtful eyes are focused to one side, as if to soften their full impact. Here is divine love embodied in human form.

EL GRECO

El Greco, as a Roman Catholic visionary and mystic, emphasizes the intersection of time with the timeless (not as Rembrandt—timeless with time). He portrays the transfiguration of human experience into the heavenly vision[85] and shows the physical going into the divine. His figures tend to turn the attention inward or upward. In *The Resurrection* all is vision and Christ floats weightless. El Greco shows the opening of heaven and men being drawn upward.

El Greco's *Christ on the Cross* is a notable example of his many powerful paintings. His are some of the most intensely emotional and expressive pictures ever created. In El Greco, color and form are used as a means of emphasizing dramatic expression, with a result that to many it is exaggeration and distortion. The figures are elongated, the limbs twisted, and strange streaks of light flash across the picture. No one else has overlaid his rhythmic forms with so fiery an orchestration of visual elements. His distortions and the departure from camera truth are not only for rhythmic and sensuous effect, but also for the truthful revelation of character. The image of Christ shows forth like an apparition, though still preserving an essentially human form in order to glorify the magnitude of his moral and physical suffering. The paintings of El Greco are filled with restless religious strife, tumult, agony, and mystic absorption.[86]

---

[85]Dixon, *Nature and Grace in Art*, pp. 167f.

[86]Dixon, *Art as Communication*, pp. 75f. Cf. also Dillenberger, *Style and Content*, p. 170.

NOLDE

Emil Nolde used color and emotion in religious painting. Many consider Nolde to be the most profound and eloquent exponent of the German Expressionist style. He has much of the excitement and inner vitality of Van Gogh. Nolde did his first religious pictures in 1909, such as *Holy Night,* using strong bright colors to build up his large figure compositions. Before the First World War he joined an expedition to the Pacific Ocean. The natives he saw there and their art made a great impression on him, and he reflected this influence in his work.[87]

Nolde was convinced that the soul of man could be made the subject of painting, and the ancient stories of the Bible probably fascinated him because they illustrate the most elementary human passions. His *Last Supper* and *Entombment* are good examples. Without any regard for artistic or other conventions, he recreated these biblical stories as they had never been painted before, in colors which did not correspond to any realistic notions. However, these paintings were able to express the excitement he himself felt and wanted to convey.[88]

A notable religious picture by Nolde is *Christ Among the Children.* A great surge of joy seems to spring from this painting. The children have rushed toward Jesus exultantly, and one has leaped into his welcoming arms. Nolde evokes emotion through color. The vivid rose, yellow, and blue express the delight of Jesus and the children at being together. The dark robes of the disciples show their disapproval of this undignified proceeding. This is one of a series which he did on the life of Christ.

ROUAULT

Georges Rouault (1871-1958) is outstanding as a Christian

---

[87]Andrew Carnduff Ritchid (ed.), *German Art of the Twentieth Century* (New York: The Museum of Modern Art, 1957), pp. 34f. Cf. also Frank and Dorothy Getlein, *Christianity and Modern Art* (Milwaukee: Bruce Publishing Co., 1961), pp. 23–42.

[88]Ibid., Getlein, p. 33.

artist. Expressionism, with its emphasis upon the rendition of subjective emotion rather than upon what is seen or upon formal relationship, finds one of its most forceful spokesmen in Rouault. As an Expressionist, he succeeded in giving life to what was centuries ago the principal concern of painters—religious art. A good example is his *Crucifixion*.[89]

Georges Rouault was a devout Christian, but his painting of Christ is not like the prettified, commercialized art which is often found in churches or shops. In expressing his ideas he used black outlines and glowing stained glass tones of somber colors. *Ecce Homo* illustrates his approach. He was rapid, intuitive, intense. He shocked by his portrayal of the dissonance and brutality of life. The few friends and lovers of painting who trusted Rouault were afraid of the direction he had taken from 1903 on. From that date there appeared figures of Christ with the face and body prodigiously deformed to express the paroxysm of the divine Passion and human cruelty. Rouault consciously turned his back on artificiality and eliminated the "prettified" or shallow.[90] An illustration of the agony of Christ is seen in *The Head of Christ*. In this agonized image, the face of Christ holds the suffering of all victims of human cruelty everywhere.[91]

Although Christian aesthetics is concerned with the arts of creation, man in the image of God, the Fall, and redemption, it finds its center of gravity in the doctrine of the Incarnation.[92] The material earth not only comes from the hand of God, but is radiant with God's presence. This means that philosophical idealism is not possible to the artist if he is to be consistent, a fact which Plato recognized. It is essential to the artist that he be free to find his meaning and expression in the material.

---

[89]Getlein, *Christianity in Modern Art,* pp. 43–58.

[90]Kuh, *Break-up,* p. 27.

[91]"Jesus As Interpreted by Master Painters," *Wisdom,* I, No. 12 (December, 1956), p. 68. Cf. also Getlein, op. cit., pp. 43–58.

[92]One category not discussed is the whole area of man's response to the great acts of God. These are his attempts to obey and adore, his service and his worship. This appears in the arts in the artist's explorations of the moral life and in his creation of the whole body of devotional and instructional arts. There are many narrative paintings included in this category.

The Christian artist goes further in seeing that physical material was also judged worthy to contain Jesus Christ. It is thus radiant with both the glory of the creation and the new creation that proceeds from the Incarnation.[93]

As has been seen, a Christian is concerned with all art that seeks to probe into the reality of God's creation. Naturalism and Expressionism can teach him much about the earth. Cubism, Abstract art, and Action painting reveal the creative power of man made in the image of God. Many Expressionists reveal man's alienation, cruelty, and despair. But Christians have the additional insight that allows them to possess a holy Naturalism. They see the special dangers of an isolated, self-centered artist and the special importance of those who would create under God and in relation to his redemptive purpose. The Christian sees tragedy not as the end of man but as the result of rebellion and as the possible seed bed of hope. Above all the Christian sees the possibility of art as celebrating the redemption focalized in Christ.[94]

---

[93]Dixon, *Nature and Grace in Art*, p. 79.
[94]Dixon, *Nature and Grace*, pp. 198–201.

Index

126

Sin 16; 22; 39
Sociology 18
Spirit 20
Standards 16; 27
Subconscious 95; 96; 112
Subjectivity 24
Suffering 37; 38; 39; 42; 62; 68; 87
Surrealism 70; 77; 95; 112; 116
Symbol 13; 19; 28; 37; 46; 52; 62;
    64; 66; 67; 81; 96; 101; 109;
    113; 114; 115
Theater of the Absurd 34; 67; 69;
    70; 71-75; 82; 87
Theater of Cruelty 70
Theology 13; 14; 17; 18; 21; 22;
    23; 31; 35; 85; 92; 98; 106
Time 20; 96; 98-99; 113; 120
Tragedy 80; 91
Tragicomedy 62; 80
Vision 24; 25; 26; 27; 30; 32; 33;
    39; 40; 44; 48; 54; 55; 67; 74;
    78; 80; 87; 91
World 18; 20; 21; 26; 29; 32; 37;
    42; 48; 49; 50; 54; 55; 57; 65;
    66
World-view 25; 26 27; 31; 36
Worship 100; 101; 102; 102; 122

128

129

130